THE CALL

God's Daughters
Empowered to Serve with
Love and Compassion

CAROLYN A. COOKS

KP PUBLISHING COMPANY

ISBN: 978-1-960001-33-7 (Paperback)
ISBN: 978-1-960001-34-4 (eBook)

Editor: Frank Williams
Cover Design: Juan Roberts, Creative Lunacy
Literary Director: Sandra Slayton James

Published by:

KP Publishing Company
Publisher of Fiction, Nonfiction & Children's Books
www.kp-pub.com

Printed in the United States of America

DEDICATION

This book is dedicated to my parents, the late Rev. Robert and Willie Mae Williamson, who brought me up under the admonition of the Lord. They gave me the most important thing parents can give to their children—they gave me Jesus!

I dedicate this book to my husband and children, who encouraged me to write a book and continued to encourage me until it was complete.

I dedicate this book to the Sisters who will read this book. I pray you will find it helpful as you journey through your "Call" into the Ministry.

By the Grace of God,
Pastor Carolyn A. Cooks

CONTENTS

Chapter 1

THE CALL

To be successful in ministry, to give yourself fully to God in this service, you must be confident of your calling. There can be no doubt in your mind that this is God's will for you. Don't allow people to cause you to doubt the call is real.

JESUS AND WOMEN

There will always be those who are still holding on to that old, antiquated way of thinking, which by the way is not scriptural, that God did not call women to preach. God is no respecter of persons.

In Galatians 3:28 (ESV) it reads,

> *"There is neither Jew or Greek,*
> *there is neither slave or free, there is neither male or female,*
> *for you are all one in Christ Jesus."*

For Jesus, there were no double standards, no limits on the gifts given to women, and no exclusions of women in ministry. Jesus came and broke down the walls of separation in every area of Christianity. There are many instances in scripture that clearly gives evidence of Jesus' involvement with women in a positive way. One of the most significant accounts in the Bible relating to this fact and cannot be overlooked, is Jesus commissioned a "woman," Mary Magdalene to carry the first proclamation of His resurrection to His Disciples: John 20:17,

> "... go to my brethren, and say unto them,
> 'I am ascending to My Father and your Father,
> and to My God and your God,"

(see also Luke 24:1-12, Matthew 28:1-10, Mark 16:9, and John 20:1-18). This leaves no room for doubt and questions regarding Jesus using women to share the Good News.

Another notable account is in St. John 4. Here the Bible gives the account of Jesus needing to go through Samaria. Jewish customs prevented them from dealing with Samaritans. Jesus' actions were clearly a statement that this custom was about to change. While at Jacob's Well in Samaria, He talked with a Samaritan woman; this was totally unheard of in those days. After a one-on-one conversation with Jesus, she was filled with the Holy Spirit and went back into the city and told them of her encounter with Jesus. Jesus had no problem with this woman going and telling people about Him. Isn't that what preachers and evangelists do? As a result of her telling them about Jesus, they believed, and Jesus remained an additional two days in the city of Samaria.

This was no coincidence!

Jesus was setting the stage for women to carry the Good News of salvation to those who did not know Him.

God chose the dynamics of preaching as the vehicle to bring the word of God to the nations. Titus 1:3 says,

*"In due time God would manifest
His Word through preaching . . ."*

God chose His sons and daughters for this service. Joel 2:28 reads,

*"And it shall come to pass afterward that I will pour out My
Spirit on all flesh; your sons and daughters shall prophesy."*

Preaching is a lifeline to those who may be drowning in their sins and who do not know Jesus. I am confident that if someone is drowning, it does not matter to them who gives them a life jacket, be they male or female.

THE GIFT OF PREACHING (PREACHERS)

When God established His church, He put all things in place. God is a God of order. In Ephesians 4:11-14 we find God clearly gave gifts to the church. These gifts are positions of responsibility, accountability, and authority. God's desire was for His church, body of believers (not a building) to be fully equipped with His Word. Those positions would be filled by people chosen by God. Preachers are part of this group that God chose for

*"the perfecting of the saints, for the work of ministry, for the
edifying of the body of Christ." Ephesians 4:12(KJV)*

Preachers are anointed and sent. Romans 10:14-15 (KJV) says,

*"How then shall they call on Him in whom
they have not believed? And how shall they believe in
Him of whom they have not heard?*

THE CALL

And how shall they hear without a preacher?
And how shall they preach unless they are sent?

We find in I Corinthians 12:1-31, the evidence of those gifts being given to us by the Holy Spirit. Because God is all knowing, He knew the gift the Holy Spirit would assign to each of us. The Bible tells us in Ephesians 1:1-14 that God chose us, predestined us, adopted us, accepted us, and sealed us before the foundation of the world according to the good pleasure of His will.

ACKNOWLEDGING YOUR CALL

When the call is real, you will experience what I call the "Jeremiah Syndrome." It will be like fire shut up in your bones. In Jeremiah 20:9,

> *"But His Word was in my heart like burning fire, shut up in my bones: I was weary of holding back and I could not."*

When God has called you and placed His Word in your heart and in your mouth, you will have no peace or satisfaction until you embrace the call and surrender yourself to God. I can assure you He will not rescind the call. As it reads in Romans 11:29 (KJV),

> *"For the gifts and the calling of God are irrevocable."*

I remember when I tried to ignore the call on my life. After all I was a female (as if God didn't know), and I knew that I would face rejection, denials, and many challenges. So, I decided to settle with being a great Sunday school teacher, which is a noble call all in itself. But that was not God's plan for my life. After much unrest in my spirit and tears, I finally said yes to the call. I realized that God would be with me, and He was more than anything or anyone against me. God did not take the gift of teaching from me; He expanded it to another level. He moved me from a room with a limited number of people to a larger forum in different church congregations to preach/teach His Word to many people. I fully trusted God to be with me and to speak through me regardless of the prevailing prejudice towards women preachers. I fully embraced Philippians 1:6,

> *"Being confident of this very thing, that He who has begun a*
> *good work in you will complete it until the day of Jesus Christ."*

The call to preach/teach comes from God. He will always be the strength of your calling. He will be the one to sustain you during those times of uncertainty. He will stand up in you when others are trying to pull you down. As for being female, God knew you and I were female before anyone else, including our parents. Before you were born, God had a plan for your life, as it reads in Psalm 139:16 (NJKV),

> *"Your eyes saw my substance, being yet unformed. And in Your*
> *book, they all were written, the days fashioned for me, When as*
> *yet there were none of them."*

Please know, my sister, you are not defined by a pulpit. If you are never invited to stand in a pulpit, it does not negate the confidence of the call on your life. You must know without a shadow of a doubt that you are a woman of God, called to preach the word of God, and that is who you are no matter where you are. Those who have a co-vocation, when you are on your secular job, regardless of the title or position you hold, you are still a preacher working in that position. The same applies when you are in the supermarket, the doctor's office or standing in line at the post office, you are still a preacher taking care of personal business. No one can take that gift from you. Claim it, own it, and walk in it!

It is important to remember that it is God's plans to open doors for you. All you have to do is prepare yourself to the best of your ability. It is up to you to be steadfast.

Jeremiah 29:11 (NIV) says,

> *"For I know the plans I have for you," declares the Lord, "plans to prosper you and not to harm you, plans to give you hope and a future."*

This is God's assurance to you, and it speaks of purpose and destiny.

The plans of the devil are to make you feel unsure, doubtful, discouraged and at times hopeless and alone. His purpose is to cause you to miss the truth of God's love and purpose for you. When those times come, and they will come, you must walk through those challenges with faith and keep your eyes focused on God and His promise that He knows the plans He has for you. He will be your source of strength, II Corinthians 4:7,

> *"But we have this treasure in earthen vessels, that the excellence of the power may be of God and not of us."*

God has chosen you for this journey. He counted you worthy and faithful to serve as one of His preachers. He will enable you. The Bible says we are to walk worthy of the calling with which you were called (Ephesians 4:1), and more importantly that you walk worthy of God (I Thessalonians 2:12). This call and this journey will not be easy. God did not promise that it would be. But He did promise that if we obey Him and keep His commandments, He will never leave or forsake us. He will be with you every step of the way. I was given a very beautiful plaque for a housewarming gift that reads "The Will of

God will never take you where the Grace of God will not keep you." That is an affirmation of faith in the will and grace of God.

There were times during my ministry when I shared the pulpit with preachers who were not pleased with my presence. They were courteous, for the most part, but very distant. I felt very uncomfortable, but I knew I was where God wanted me to be.

Being female, I never assumed that I would be welcomed in all church pulpits. For that reason, I would always sit in the congregation unless I was invited by the pastor of that particular church to join him and the clergy on the podium. Most times after I acknowledged the invitation I would choose to remain in the congregation. As I stated earlier, I never felt that I was defined by a pulpit or where I sat in a church.

During my ministry, I was invited to preach at three relatively well-known churches, where I was the first female to preach from their church pulpit. That was clearly the hand of God at work.

Your calling is not about your gender. However, the reality is for some it is still an issue. It is not my intent to present this book as a platform of gender bias. However, my intention is to cover any area in the ministry where you may face challenges, and to encourage you to not allow them to hinder your service to God and His people.

So, I say to you, my sister, what the Apostle Paul told Timothy,

"Stir up the gift of God that is in you." II Timothy 1:6

Always remain confident of your calling. Don't allow doubters or dissidents to discourage you. These groups have always been around and will always be present. Remember, Jesus had His and I say that you are in good company.

Preach the word, my sister, and may the grace of God carry you through your ministry and be blessed!

Chapter 2

MY STORY / JOURNEY

I grew up in a small town in Louisiana, the daughter of a Baptist pastor. In our home, church was the only option. From Sunday school through B.Y.P.U., my Sundays were spent at church.

As a young person, Sunday school was always my favorite part of church. I enjoyed having to learn memory verses and reciting them in class. Even as an adult, Sunday school continues to be my favorite part of church followed closely by Bible study.

It was during one of those Bible study classes (Through The Bible) taught by my pastor, at that time, that the word of God came alive to me. We were encouraged to purchase a Scofield Reference Bible. The word of God was opened up to me in a way that it had never been before. In addition to homework assignments, I would spend hours reading and learning the true meanings of Bible topics such as redemption, justification, salvation, the Holy Spirit and dispensations, along with so many other doctrinal truths. I developed a hunger for the word of God that remains to this day.

After attending a Sunday school teacher's training seminar, I was assigned to work with one of the seasoned teachers at my home church. After she resigned, the class was assigned to me. Later, I was reassigned to teach the young adult class. I realized that I needed formal education to be able to efficiently teach young adults. I enrolled into a local Christian Bible College where I received a certificate in teaching.

During my time in college, my home church held a service, "the week of prayer," when the chairman asked for a volunteer to do the lesson for the third night. The Spirit prompted me to volunteer, and I did. From that time, I began to be invited to speak at my home church for its Women's Day programs, Ushers' Day Programs, and to teach Bible study occasionally. Eventually, I began to be invited to speak at other local churches for the same type of services.

After graduation, I began to feel the Lord calling me to preach. I was afraid. By then both of my parents had passed and went home to be with the Lord and I felt that I had no one to talk to about what was happening to me. After many sleepless nights and unrest in my spirit, I experienced what I call my "encounter with God." Finally, when I could no longer deny the call I sensed on my life to preach, I acknowledged it and shared the news with my pastor, who was not surprised. He encouraged me to move forward and several months later, he licensed me to preach.

At the beginning of my journey in ministry, I did not have the full support of my entire family. Beginning with my husband who could not believe that God would use an ordinary person like me to carry His Word. It wasn't until after God had continually used me to preach at our annual Ushers' Day and Women's Day programs that he began to slowly embrace the possibility that this calling could be real. Perhaps it was because of the traditional opinion that God did not call women to preach or maybe it was because he did not want to be part of this mission, after all he did not marry a preacher. Whatever his reason, the reality was, I was sure of the call and continued to be used by God in spite of the personal difficulties I had to endure.

Thank God, my husband became one of my greatest supporters.

My Children: Before I was officially licensed, I talked with each one of my children, individually, to find out how they felt about having a "Preacher Mama." Thank God they all embraced the idea. Neither one of them expressed sadness or unhappiness because of my position. I was told if that's what God wanted me to do, to go ahead and do it. Thank God for the support of my children. Disapproval from them was not one of the many battles I had to fight in order to fulfill God's calling in my life. However, they did encounter some opinions which were not favorable from some of their friends. One of their friends had the audacity to tell one of my sons that God did not call women to preach, and that God was going to punish his father (my husband) for allowing me to preach. I told my son not to respond to him or anyone else for that matter that voiced negative opinions about me. They were not expected to defend my call, just exhibit a "wait and see God work" attitude.

My Parents: Neither of my parents lived to see me licensed and later ordained in the ministry. I'm not absolutely sure how my dad would have reacted. I can only say that he was from the generation that did not embrace women in the pulpit.

A few months before his passing, he had the opportunity to hear me speak at an Ushers' Day program. After the service he told me that I had done well. This was before I acknowledged my call to preach as I was just a "speaker."

It meant so much to me to know that my father thought I had done well.

I often think of my father and how he would have reacted to my being called to pastor a church. I can only hope that he would have accepted it. After all he was the parent who would sit down with me and discuss the Bible on the occasions when he visited me at my home. He called me "Annie." I can still hear him say, "Annie get your book," referring to the Bible. He would proceed to discuss different passages of scripture with me. We would sit for long periods of time just the two of us enjoying the Word of God. I believe that since he is home with the Lord, who is no respecter of persons, that my dad is finally proud of the daughter whom he taught to love the Word of God, the daughter that God called to preach!

My mother, on the other hand, was always present to support me when I was invited to speak. My older sister and my brother would bring her to the service. She would always, without fail, have encouraging words to say to me afterwards. I know that she was proud of me and embraced my being used by God to speak and teach His Word.

My Siblings: My younger sister confessed to me at one of our family breakfasts' that at first, she did not accept my call because according to her our dad had expressed to her that women were not called to preach. It was much later after I continued to preach that she finally believed that I was being "real." She witnessed the sincerity and dedication I exhibited and because she knew that I was not, in her words, a "phony" person, she accepted that I indeed had been called to preach. I also know that it was God who changed her heart.

Two of my siblings never showed anything but support, as I said earlier my oldest sister, and my youngest brother. In the absence of my parents, they were both present when I graduated from Bible college the first time. My youngest brother was my greatest supporter. He was also an ordained minister, and my right hand. We shared so many hours on the phone or in person discussing God, His goodness, and His Word. My brother was there for me during all my ups and downs. He was the shoulder I could cry on when I needed support.

My second oldest sister never expressed an opinion one way or the other. I believe she was in the "wait-and-see" mode. However, without saying it, she also accepted my call into ministry. She would call me for help with her spiritual questions regarding faith and unforgiveness, etc. She trusted my answers and followed my advice when given. She would always tell me that I was "different." I believe that I was instrumental in some of the decisions she made regarding her walk with God.

To God be the glory!

My Beginning/Past experiences: Unfortunately, I did not have a female mentor to turn to for help. I didn't know any female preachers that I felt close enough to personally, someone to talk to, to ask questions, seek advice and directions from. That is not to say that there were not any, I just didn't know any personally. That is the primary reason I was compelled to write this book, to share my experiences with young women who have been called to preach, teach, and perhaps pastor.

I had male mentors, two former pastors and one pastor who had preceeded my pastorate by two or three years. I must say they were all very kind and helpful to me. They were all available to share their experiences and knowledge with me and to advise me in matters of church administration. NOTE: It is equally important to share with you that I had much respect and love for their wives, too. I purposely established a respectful and genuine relationship with them—genuine being the *key* word. Whenever I had an opportunity to publicly thank those pastors, I also recognized their wives and thanked them for their support as well. I would strongly suggest you do the same.

However, being male they could not help me with the dress code, make up, proper pulpit etiquette for females, or how to mix motherhood with ministry.

They could not tell me how to balance preparing dinner, doing housework, and attending parent conferences as well as preaching. Only a female who had experienced those things would be able to help me in those areas. Only a female who could relate to the experience would be able to share in my hurt and rejection. Only a female could tell me how to handle these and other situations with grace and dignity.

After being installed as a pastor, I was fortunate to be invited to a group called The Reverend Sisters. There I met women of God in various ministries. Some who had been doing the work of Christ for a long time. I cannot tell you how I felt being embraced by so many women of God who could share and perhaps help shape me for the journey I was now embarking upon as a pastor. They were very warm and accepting. It was there that I found how well we could come together and support one another. Hearing accounts of support and rejection they had encountered greatly influenced and encouraged me. To know there was a place where I could go and express myself honestly without being judged or criticized was a blessing for me. Among them were years of experience being shared that all young women, or those new in the ministry, should be exposed to. Listening, sharing, and learning from them is a course that you won't find being offered in seminary. It was there that I met some women who have become my closest friends. We formed close ties and continue to support each other. We pray together, shop and have lunch as friends and supporters of each other.

One of my personal affirmations comes from I Timothy 1:12 which says,

"I thank Christ Jesus our Lord, who has enabled me, because
He counted me faithful, putting me into the ministry."

Again, I hope that you will find this book helpful to you as you journey through your ministry. There are many scriptures included in this book to encourage you in your walk in ministry. Embrace the truths of these scriptures and use them as a point of reference and a refreshing when in doubt.

I am honored to be able to share my experiences, including my mistakes, with you, to perhaps help you on the most important journey you will ever take.

Go forward and be blessed!

Chapter 3

SHORING UP THE CALL

Shoring up means to give support to. There are what I call the three "C's" of ministry that comes with the call. These three elements are very important for supporting or shoring up the call. They are:

    A.   Character

    B.   Confidence

    C.   Commitment

These three things must be developed as you move forward in your service to God as His preachers. We will explore each one individually.

Character: Character defines who you really are as a person. It defines your disposition by openly displaying your thoughts by your actions. Kind thoughts produce kind actions, as does patience, self-control, and goodness.

The Bible is filled with scriptures admonishing us how and why good character is inherent to us being created in the image of God. I challenge you to find any place in the Bible where God or Jesus displayed bad character.

Even though they both got angry at times, their anger, unlike ours, was always justified. Neither one was ever rude, selfish, or unkind to anyone. We are to imitate their character.

Good character can be attributed to the fruit of the Spirit found in Galatians 5:22-23,

> *"But the fruit of the Spirit is love, joy, peace, longsuffering,*
> *kindness, goodness faithfulness, gentleness, self-control."*

Each of these components are contributors to good character. Self-control, kindness, gentleness, longsuffering, and faithfulness are all associated with a person's attitude towards others. Good character is indicative of a humble spirit. In Romans 12:3,

> *"For I say, through the grace given to me, to everyone who is*
> *among you, not to think of himself more highly than he ought*
> *to think, but to think soberly, as God has dealt to each one a*
> *measure of faith."*

Humility leads to wisdom, takes advice, and ends in honor. James 4:10 says,

> *"Humble yourself in the sight of the Lord*
> *and He will lift you up."*

God is glorified when we imitate His character. Matthew 5:16 reads this way,

> *"Let your light so shine before men that they may see your good*
> *works and glorify your father in heaven."*

Your gift in the ministry is an honor from God. He did not place you in this position to become selfish, prideful, and conceited. Pride leads to disgrace and destruction and ends in downfall.

There is an account in the book of Il Chronicles 26, citing the exploits of King Uzziah. He began with the right spirit and attitude. However, he developed some character flaws, began to listen to people rather than God. He became puffed up with pride, lost his humility, and died outside of the will and grace of God. There is an old saying, "It's not how you start but, how you finish."

Whatever you do , my sister, don't become:

1. Unapproachable
2. Unteachable
3. Unreliable
4. Ungrateful
5. Resentful
6. Rebellious
7. Prideful

Good character improves as you consistently demonstrate obedience to God and He will bless you in your ministry. Remember you are God's representative. Put your best character forward.

Confidence: Your confidence does not come from arrogance. It comes from God through your faith in Him. He will supply the courage and confidence that you will need to carry you through any uncertain situation. Again, we turn to the word of God.

Proverbs 3:5-6 says,

"Trust in the Lord with all your heart, and lean not on your own understanding, In all your ways acknowledge Him, and He will direct your paths."

In Luke 4:16-30, we find Jesus expounding on His mission/ assignment from God. He stated it with complete confidence, knowing what was expected of Him. He was determined to fulfill every aspect of His mission. However, He was not without challenges. In Luke 4:22, Nazareth, where He grew up, the people from there could not accept His pronouncement of His assignment because they thought they *knew* Him. They *knew* of Him by way of His earthly parents, earthly siblings, economic status, and limited formal education: They *knew* He had not matriculated from the University of Nazareth or any other prestigious Christian school. Even though they had heard of His miracles in Capernaum, they just couldn't accept the fact that "Joseph's boy" could do all these things. Jesus met this challenge with confidence. He didn't allow their opinions to cause Him to waiver in His confidence, or lose sight of His mission. He knew there were too many people who would benefit from Him fulfilling the purpose of His mission and He was not about to allow a handful of naysayers stop or slow Him down. He never lost faith in His ability to carry out the duties of His mission. Since the assignment came from His Father, Jesus was confident that God would give him power to complete the work He came to do. This is an example for you.

Godly confidence also comes from experience. Sometimes God will allow you to go through a trial to test you, so that you will know experientially God's care and deliverance from your trial. You will then be able to confidently witness to others your personal experience. I Peter 3:15-16,

> *"But sanctify the Lord God in your hearts, and always be ready*
> *to give a defense to everyone who asks you a reason for the hope*
> *that is in you, with meekness and fear."*

In the Bible you will find accounts of various people who were chosen by God to go through unbelievable trials. In Genesis 22, we find the account of Abraham's test regarding Isaac. Here Abraham proved his confidence in God's promise and His Word.

You, too, must have complete confidence in the word of God. You must believe it, study it, obey it, uphold it, and promote it. God's Word is our lifeline to Him. And let us not forget there is no new written word from God though He speaks to us and daily gives us downloads for our walk. What God wants us to know has already been written. He has given us sixty-six books to have as a testimony of who He is, what He does, and how He loves and protects those who belong to Him.

The more time you spend in His Word, the more you'll get to know Him. You will grow closer to Him and more confident as you read of His love, forgiveness, kindness, provision, protection, and deliverance, etc. In the Bible, you will find in Isaiah 40:8, *"The grass withers, the flowers fades, but the word of our God stands forever."* Therein is your confidence in Him, His Word, and His promise to be with us on this journey that He planned for our lives. Thus, your confidence will be developed as you find encouragement from His Word and the Holy Spirit that lives in you.

You must be confident in the reason for your ministry; to reach those in need of salvation.

God has a plan of salvation for all who will believe in His Son Jesus Christ. This message of salvation is necessary for us to make an intelligent decision to follow Christ, who purchased our salvation on the cross of Calvary.

Commitment: I Corinthians 4:2 says,

> *"Moreover it is required in stewards*
> *that one be found faithful."*

Your faith in God supports your commitment to God. Webster defines commitment as (1) an act of committing to a charge or trust (2) the state of being obligated or emotionally impelled."

Again, from the account of Jesus in Luke 4:16-30 we find Jesus as a perfect example of commitment. Jesus was committed to His mission—totally committed. He was first of all, committed to His Father who had given Him the mission. Secondly, He was committed to the fulfillment of His mission. Even to the death on the cross. Because of His commitment, He didn't back down, run away, or stop when situations became hard. He was determined to stay the course. Jesus didn't get halfway through and decide it was too time consuming, too difficult, or too dangerous. He was committed, and He knew that God would always be with Him.

Your level of commitment must never be questionable. In the course of a lifetime, we all commit to many things; relationships, jobs, political causes, family, church activities, and most importantly to God. 1 Corinthians 15:58

> *"Therefore, my beloved brethren, be ye steadfast, immovable,*
> *always abounding in the work of the Lord, knowing that your*
> *labor is not in vain in the Lord."*

When you fully embrace the richness of that scripture, it will become your bridge over troubled water, when you run into difficulties and perhaps begin to doubt your effectiveness. God sees and honors your commitment. Another scripture to embrace is
Hebrews 6:10—12,

> *"For God is not unjust to forget your work and labor of love*
> *which you have shown toward His name, in that you have*
> *ministered to the saints and do minister. And we desire that*
> *each one of you show the same diligence to*

the full assurance of hope until the end that you do not become
sluggish but imitate those who through faith
and patience inherit the promise."

Your love for God will compel you to keep striving to offer your greatest service.

There may be times when the outlook may seem bleak, but I encourage you to keep forging ahead. With God on your side there will always be a light at the end of the tunnel.

There were times in my ministry when I felt as if I would not be able to continue, with the stress of the pastorate and having to stand alone many times on difficult issues. However, when I thought about what Jesus endured for me at Calvary, my situation paled in comparison. Besides, I never wanted to fail God, that my greatest fear.

Knowing that God considered me worthy to carry His Word still humbles me today. The scripture the Holy Spirit led me to for my installation service was John 15:16,

"You did not choose Me, but I chose you and
appointed you that you should go and bear fruit,
and that your fruit should remain, that whatever you ask the
Father in My name He may give you."

Being chosen by God to bear fruit means He sees me as capable with His help. His faith in me keeps me committed to Him.

Being committed to God also means being available and willing to serve Him at any cost. Your commitment to serve God faithfully may cost you some friends and sometime even family who are not at the level of commitment you are, and they just don't quite understand your time is not your time anymore—it belongs to God.

Being committed means you may have to step outside your comfort zone sometimes to achieve goals that will take you from one level of ministry to another. But, keep in mind, God knows where you are at all times. He will not allow you to be in a place (mentally or physically) that will bring harm to you, or that He hasn't prepared you for. Your commitment to God will bring you face to face with many challenges, but it will also bring you through those challenges.

One of the most important components of your commitment includes:

Educational Preparation:
Psalm 78:72,

> *"So he shepherded them according to the integrity of his heart and guided them by the skillfulness of his hands."*

After the call has been acknowledged and embraced by you, the next step is preparation for the journey. The previous scripture implies that it's good to have the desire, but equally important is the skill and knowledge. There is more to preaching / teaching than standing and talking. You must know what you are talking about, and how to present it.

For some of you, four years at a seminary may be financially challenging. For some it may be practically impossible. However, there are many reputable Bible colleges that are affordable and offer an excellent curriculum. Additionally, there are on-line classes offered by experienced, well known, and trusted pastors. The point is that as you prepare yourself spiritually and personally, you must also prepare yourself intellectually as well.

It will be helpful to know:

1. Bible Hermeneutics: The science of interpreting the Holy Scriptures of the Old and New Testaments.
2. Homiletics: The science and study of the method of preparing and delivering sermons. It will also be helpful to study Systematic Theology and Expository Preaching.

You will need tools:

1. A good Study Bible
2. At least one additional Bible Translation
3. A set of good Bible Commentaries
4. Concordance
5. Bible Dictionary
6. Language Dictionary
7. Other resources for additional clarity and understanding

You will need to be:

1. Committed to studying and embracing the truths of the entire Bible.
2. Fully prepared with an intelligent understanding of the saving grace of God's Word.

With the existence of technology, Biblical information is more readily available to everyone. However, some of it is theologically unsound and compromised. This is another reason to acquire a good education.

II Timothy 2:15,

> *"Study to show thyself approved unto God, a workman that needs not to be ashamed, rightly dividing the word of truth."*

As carriers of God's Word, it is our responsibility to know and teach the absolute truth, without wavering or compromising.

When you have done your very best to prepare yourself, the holy Spirit will do His part in assisting you. You can count on it. We honor our commitment to God by fully acknowledging and embracing the need to grow and improve in order to give Him our best. Proverbs 4:7 says,

> *"Wisdom is the principle thing; Therefore get wisdom*
> *and in all your getting, get understanding."*

Remember my sister, character, confidence and commitment are all part of your call. It is important my sister, that you exhibit and practice these things to shore up your call as one of God's preaching daughters. Go forward and be a blessing!

Chapter 4

ON BEING "YOU"

We live in a world where advertisers spend billions of dollars trying to convince you that you are NOT okay the way that you are. Their job is to make you believe that you should be better and you will improve by using their products. If allowed they would decide for you your size, your weight, the color of your eyes and hair. Even though these physical improvements are suggested, their main thrust is to get inside of your head and have you believe the hype. The Bible says in Proverbs 23:7,

"For as he thinks in his heart, so is he."

So, if you can be convinced that you need to improve you, if you are not sure of who you are, you will fall for all the hype.

Although we have discussed character in another chapter, we will make it more personal in this chapter. The first thing I would say to you my sister is "just be you." By that I mean don't try to be like anyone else. There are many powerful women of God that I admire greatly. However, I would not be true to myself or free to allow God to develop me if I tried to be someone else.

Psalm 139:14 says,

> *"I will praise You, for I am fearfully and wonderfully made."*

This scripture is not just referring to our physical appearance, but our minds as well. We are so wonderfully created that we are all wonderfully unique. No one has your DNA. You may resemble someone in your family, but the truth is you are unique and one of a kind. That was God's plan. He has created us individually to use His gift in each of us to His glory.

I Peter 4:10 says,

> *"As each one has received a gift, minister it to one another, as good stewards of the manifold grace of God."*

When God called you, He knew you just as you were. He knew your name, your personality, your family history, your character, yet He called you anyway. That is an indication that God called you as YOU—not you trying to be someone else. The word of God says in Matthew 10:30 (KJV),

> *"He knows us so well that the hairs on our heads are numbered."*

Yes, my sisters, He even knows what's under that wig or weave and yet, He called you."

Learn to accept and celebrate your uniqueness. Throughout the Bible, God used people with unique personalities and styles to do special work for the kingdom like John the Baptist. In Matthew 3:1,4

> *"In those days John the Baptist came*
> *preaching in the wilderness of Judea,"*
> *"Now John himself was clothed in camel's hair,*

*with a leather belt around his waist; and his food
was locusts and wild honey."*

John was unique and had his own style. Yet he was comfortable in his difference and totally focused on his mission because John knew who he was.

John's father was high priest, Zacharias. He dressed in a special priestly robe to perform his duties. His service was done inside the temple. His dress and duties and John's were as different as night is from day. Their callings were unique to them, and they performed their duties according to the leading of the Holy Spirit. This father and son were very different, yet both were called to serve God in a way that was planned by God for each of them.

I have learned by observation, that my personal preacher friends have their own style.

One is very animated. She moves all over the place as she preaches. Another one is very reserved, she barely moves during her message, even her voice is very controlled. One of my sister friends I call radical as her style is very contemporary. Her topics are very timely, sometimes to the point, in my opinion, of being very risky. She pulls it off very naturally. Even the order of service is very contemporary. But it works for her, it fits her personality. Another one even has a "hoop" which has a stirring factor to it that is unique to the Baptist tradition. One of my colleagues would always include a comical story in her message. I tried that but it didn't work for me. My style is more teaching than preaching and still God uses all of us. We are God's preaching daughters delivering His Word to those in need of salvation. We all respect each other as women of God that bring honor to His name. But we are not trying to imitate or judge each other's style.

One of my former pastors had a particular song that the choir would sing as he approached the pulpit. I always thought it was great to begin with a special song before the message began. The problem for me was that I could never think of a song that I felt comfortable trying to lead or sing, so there went that plan of mine. Which goes along with the truth, you can't manipulate the Spirit by trying to do what someone else does.

If you are new in the ministry, and you're not sure what your preaching style is, just continue to preach and allow God to use your gift freely. Your style will develop without trying to manipulate it or define it. God wants to use the person that He called-NOT an imposter. One of my friends shared with me that she always wanted to be like Juanita Bynum. The Spirit told her He already had a Juanita Bynum, He needed her to be herself.

Whatever your style of preaching is, always include love and warmth. Don't present yourself as being so "holy" that you seem to be above the people. You should relate to your congregation on a congenial basis. A smile is always a good place to begin. When you are comfortable in yourself that will translate to the congregation. That is why good character is so important. As I said earlier, just be you, and let the Holy Spirit do the rest. You will never know your strengths and weaknesses trying to be someone else. And whatever you do never try to impress people concerning your abilities and qualifications or compare yourself to anyone else.

My greatest experience and lesson came on the occasion of being nominated to receive recognition as one of the candidates for the "Top Ladies of Distinction" an organization of professional women who serve the community in different capacities in and around the Los Angeles area.

When I arrived at the hotel where the presentations were being held, we were given a program. Inside the program were the bios of all the candidates. When I read of their degrees, the colleges they graduated from and the community organizations they were involved with, I felt inadequate and out of place with only my certificate from the Bible college I graduated from. We were each asked to present a fifteen to twenty-minute sermon. I decided to make sure my sermon was exceptional because I felt I needed to prove myself to be as great as the other recipients. I tried to add unwritten dialog to my message and adlib as I went along and I felt very uncomfortable. Afterwards one of the members of my church mentioned that I seemed very nervous and at times a little uncertain regarding the text.

The worst was yet to come. That night as I was praying, all of a sudden, the tears began to roll down my face as I cried uncontrollably. I didn't know why I was crying. The Spirit reminded me of what I had done earlier that day at the awards' ceremony during my presentation. I was so broken in my spirit. It was then that I realized I had disappointed God by not being myself and allowing Him to use me at His will. I immediately asked God to forgive me and promised Him that I would never again compare the gift that He had given to me to anyone else's. Needless to say, I learned through that mistake that God wanted me to be me, the woman that He had called to preach His Word and pastor His people. I can honestly say that I never again tried to impress anyone or compare myself to anyone. I am me and I am God-approved!

Ephesians 2:10 (KJV) says,

> *"For we are His workmanship, created in Christ Jesus*
> *for good works, which God prepared*
> *beforehand that we should walk in them."*

We bless and encourage others when we know who we are and are being ourselves.

In the book of Daniel, we find the account of the Jews being taken captive by King Nebuchadnezzar and carried to Babylon. Included in this captivity were Daniel and his three friends. Part of the king's plans was to change their Hebrew names to pagan names. However, Daniel and his friends knew what their Hebrew names represented, so they refused to accept the name change because they knew who they were. They did not compromise to be accepted by the king and the Babylonian society. The principle on which they stood was their faith. Faith in the promise and power of God to sustain them as they remained faithful to who they were.

Your faith in God will enable you to overcome the temptation of trying to fit into the world's opinion of who you are or who you should be. You must be confident in your own identity.

When God sees you, He sees:

1. Himself—we are made in His image, we are born with the capacity to love, have compassion, etc. All of which are a duplicate of Him.
2. His greatest creation—when God created the world and everything in it, He called it good. When He created you and me, His humane creation, He called it "very good."
3. He sees a person of integrity. Not perfect but one with the capacity to mature intellectually.
4. He sees great beauty—beauty that He created.

Your identity in Christ completes you. You do not have to try to be someone else. Just let God develop you to become the woman of God that He already sees you as. Your gift was especially designed for you. God had a need for someone like you or He would never have called you. Apostles Paul and Peter were called to minister to two different groups of believers.

Paul to the Gentiles and Peter to the Jews. They met the needs of the group they had been assigned to. God used them mightily with both having their own distinct personalities and capabilities.

Walk in the destiny God has prepared for your life. Free yourself of the temptation to try to imitate someone else. There is an old proverb "To thine own self be true."

Keep your relationship with Jesus as your top priority. Grow in your spirit and knowledge of God and allow God to do the rest. And remember— just be you!

Chapter 5

THE IMPORTANCE OF PRAYER

As Christians we have been given a perpetual invitation to come boldly to God in prayer as it says in Hebrews 4:16,

> *"Let us therefore come boldly unto the throne of grace, that we may obtain mercy, and find grace to help in time of need."*

It has already been established that prayer is our vehicle of communication to God. It is the vehicle that has been provided for us freely by God. As we search the scriptures, we find the prophets prayed, and most importantly Jesus prayed.

The most important element in your ministry is your prayer life. Spending time in prayer is imperative for your strength. That strength includes knowing you live under the covering of His presence, given refuge and protection from the enemy and reassurance that you don't have to be afraid (see Psalm 91). Spending time with God in prayer is an outward expression of an inward desire to be in His presence and seeking His guidance. For us, dear sisters in ministry, prayer time with God is absolutely necessary.

ESTABLISHING A PERSONAL RELATIONSHIP

Above everything else, God desires a close personal relationship with each of His children. Through prayer God purposes to establish and deepen your personal relationship with Him. It is impossible to develop this kind of relationship without spending significant time with Him alone in prayer.

I compare the concept of spending time alone with God establishing your relationship with Him to establishing your personal relationship with your spouse or significant other. You desire private, intimate time together. You don't want anyone to be with you in your personal time alone, not even your best friend. The more time you spend together, the better you get to know each other and the closer you get in your relationship. This is how we establish a loving, trusting relationship with God, by spending quality time alone with Him. Time alone with God is the place where you can be vulnerable and transparent with Him as you speak out to Him from the depth of your heart. Although He already knows every one of our thoughts, His desire is to hear from you. There is an indelible connection in the space and quiet time with you and the Father.

Prayer is the way you get to know God, not just know about Him. Most people have heard about God and consequently know about Him. But they have no personal relationship with God.

Through your personal relationship with God, you will experience power to withstand the temptations and trials that are part of your ministry. You will also be able to hear God's voice more clearly as He speaks to you. Through prayer, seek His directions as you navigate through the plans He has for you like it states in Jeremiah 29:11,

"For I know the plans I have for you" declares the Lord,
"plans to prosper you and not to harm you, plans to
give you hope and a future."

A personal relationship with God will give you a clear understanding that you are in the right place at the right time on His scheduled plans for you. It is important that you stay focused on God's plans for you and praying for His guidance is the key to success. Through prayer you will have a deeper understanding about forgiveness for yourself as well as for others. You will not be able to keep your relationship with God in order with unforgiveness in your heart. From Matthew 6:14-15,

"For if you forgive men their trespasses, your heavenly Father
will also forgive you. But if you do not forgive men their
trespasses, neither will your Father forgive your trespasses."

Pray that your heart will be united with God. Sometimes your heart will be torn in so many directions, you won't be sure where to place your concentration. This is when you ask God to unite your heart to His asking that He will give you godly wisdom to make the best decisions.

Your relationship with God will cause you to understand that your time spent in prayer with Him is not a daily duty but a strong desire for His presence.

COMMITMENT

Your personal time with God is a commitment to your personal relationship with Him.

You will not be able to develop a powerful prayer life without committing to a regular time alone with God. Whatever you do , don't ever feel as if prayer is a duty. It is a privilege to be able to talk to God at anytime, anywhere, about anything. It is to your advantage to desire prayer time alone with God.

Please be aware that if your commitment to prayer is not absolute, Satan will pressure you out of its daily practice. You will find yourself so busy, even with good things, that you might neglect your prayer time.

Luke 10: 38-42 says this,

> *"Now it happened as they went that He entered a certain village; and a certain woman named Martha welcomed Him into her home And she had a sister called Mary, who also sat at Jesus' feet and heard His Word. But Martha was distracted with much serving, and she approached Him and said "Lord, do You not care that my sister has left me to serve alone? Therefore tell her to help me." And Jesus answered and said to her "Martha, Martha, you are worried and troubled about many things. But one thing is needed, and Mary has chosen that good part, which will not be taken away from her."*

Set some time to have your phone on voice mail so that you will not be disturbed and can retrieve your calls at a later time. You might also inform your friends of your set time with God expecting them to respect your request not to be disturbed at that particular time. In I Thessalonians 5:17,

> *"Pray without ceasing,"*

means we do not allow long periods of time without spending quality, intimate time with God in prayer. Even though your schedule may be extremely busy or filled, you must make time for prayer. Without daily prayer, you are likely to explode by the stress of your busy schedule. Prayer time is also a time to be silent before God, listening for His voice, and following His directions. It's been my experience when I make time for God, He always gives me time to do whatever I need to do. Time in prayer with God gives you peace, a clear mind, and power to persevere under all circumstances.

Stay committed to your personal prayer time with God.

BALANCE

You must also have a balanced prayer life. There are different types of prayer. The major kinds of prayer are:

A. **Confession:** Especially important in the area of sin as it reads in I John 1:9,

> *"If we confess our sins, He is faithful and just to forgive us our sins and to cleanse us from all unrighteousness."*

Most of us have done or said things in our past that did not find favor with God. Don't be in denial about past experiences that may need to be confessed.

B. **Praise and Thanksgiving:** Praise God for who He is (Psalm 93) and for what He does for His people (Psalm 104).
Thank Him for your life as echoed in Hebrews 13:15, Ephesians 5:20, and I Thessalonians 5:18.

Have a time of prayer when all you do is thank God for who He is and the blessings and favor He has bestowed upon you. Time spent in thanksgiving blesses God and demonstrates to him that He is more than just someone to turn to when you are in trouble. Imagine you had a child and the only time that you heard from them was when they needed something from you. No doubt after a while you would feel that your relationship was predicated on what you could do for them. God is our Father so, imagine how He must feel when He only hears from you when you need something from Him.

C. **Intercession:** Prayer concerning others (see Ephesians 1:15-19). As you search the scriptures, you will find those whom God chose to use also prayed on behalf of others. David prayed not only for himself but for others also as in Psalm 85:4-9. Moses prayed often for the Israelites as they journeyed from Egypt to the Promised Land, Hezekiah prayed as recorded in 2Kings 19:14-19, and our Savior Jesus Christ prayed for us (see John 17:20-23).

D. **Petition and Supplication:** The largest category of prayers in the Bible which includes petitioning for God's mercy, grace, and help (see Philippians 4:6-7). It will always be comforting to know that our God is a faithful, loving, trustworthy God filled with grace and mercy.

E. **Personal and community prayers:** Personal prayer will lead to a greater understanding of His will for your life (Psalm 139:23-24: 143:8,10).
Community prayer joins your heart to others in petitioning God on behalf of the nation, your community and your church. I Timothy 2:1-4,

> *"Therefore I exhort first of all that supplications, prayers, intercession, and giving of thanks be made for all men, for Kings and all who are in authority, that we may lead a quiet*

and peaceable life in all godliness and reverence, For this is good and acceptable in the sight of God our Savior, who desires all men to be saved and to come to the knowledge of the truth."

PRAYER PARTNERS

In your prayer life, it is important to have a prayer partner. Someone who you trust and feel their spirit. Someone who will encourage you and support you especially during your time of trials. Someone you feel comfortable in sharing your heart and concerns with, being confident that your information will not be shared with anyone else. Before choosing a prayer partner, pray and ask God to lead you to someone who sincerely believes in the power of prayer, someone who truly believes in God.

PREPARING YOUR MESSAGES

As you prepare your message, always pray first. Ask God for guidance and the words of wisdom that will speak reality and truth into the lives of the hearers. When you request God's divine guidance, He will provide you with the ability to prepare messages that will be easily understood and received by the hearers. When you ask God for assistance and directions, it pleases God.

Remember, you are the messenger, the Message should be from the heart of God.

PRAYER AND FAITH

When David prayed in Psalm 40, he prayed and waited for God to answer his prayer. "I waited patiently for the Lord." It is important to understand that God does not work on your time schedule. Quite often there is a waiting period. It's doing the waiting period that your faith in God increases (see Isaiah. 40:31). Sometimes faith looks ridiculous to those who don't have it. But keep waiting in Faith.

Many times, when we pray, we already have a pre-determined way we want God to answer our prayer. And more often than not, if the answer doesn't come when we want it, the way we want it, we already have a plan "B" just in case and this kind of prayer shows no faith in God to answer our prayers according to His will, which is always for our absolute good.

You must operate in the faith realm. Remember delays are not denials. Learn to wait on God's answer., and while you wait, continue to thank Him for His love for you.

In 2001, I had a bad experience with sciatica. This illness lasted for approximately eight months and during those months of intense pain, I continued to pray and thank God for my healing as if it had already occurred. Needless to say, my healing came. My faith in God never wavered.

Prayer is the catalyst that will propel you forward in anything that you do. Whatever you desire to do in your service to God should be preceded by prayer. When anyone attempts to accomplish anything, if prayer doesn't come first—or worst yet—if prayer is not included at all, then it's the flesh at work. It is all about what you can do by yourself apart from God. When that kind of attitude is embraced, failure is inevitable.

Remember, without a close relationship with God which includes prayer for guidance, you have no ministry so, why not let Him lead you.

I Thessalonians 5:17—18 (KJV) it says,

"Pray without ceasing. In everything give thanks for this is the will of God in Christ Jesus concerning you."

Chapter 6

CULTIVATING RELATIONSHIP

(Navigating Through Ministry Hang-Ups)

There are three things among us ladies that we don't like to discuss—but it is a reality: it's ugly, but true. They are discontent, envy and people pleasing. Very few of us will admit it, but if the truth be told, all of us have had our time with them. How many of us in our time of discontent have wished for a T.V. ministry, or be a best-selling author or pastor a megachurch? We've all had the desire to move to at least one of those levels. We must, however, realize that the journey that God has planned for you will be according to His Master plan. You may never gain national notoriety or fame. People may never know your name beyond your local community. But God knows exactly who you are and exactly where you are at all times. And in the end, if we fulfill our destiny that God has for each of us, we will have done what God planned for us. Let's consider three things that could potentially be "hang-ups" as you navigate through your call into the ministry.

DISCONTENT

Zechariah 4:10 (NLT) says,

"Do not despise this small beginning, for the Lord rejoices to see the work begin . . ."

There will always be a need for ministry to people who do not feel they fit in with a megachurch but will be faithful members in a small congregation.

There are a great number of women preachers, pastors, and evangelists that serve God faithfully in small settings with small memberships. On any given Sunday, pulpits are filled with women pastors in hotels, storefronts, halls, and rented buildings who are being used by God to minister to a group of people who need the word of God. The true blessing is that God has chosen us to proclaim His Word to a dying world. The blessing is two-fold: for us and for those that we serve. That is the key word "serve." We have to see ourselves as "servants" of God. Our greatest desire is to hear God say to us, "Well done, good and faithful servant."

Perhaps your call is to be a great assistant to someone. There is a very special need for dedicated assistant pastors, youth ministry leaders, as well as leaders for various ministries within the church establishment. In his book, "Building Credibility in Leadership Principles for Secondary Leaders," Michael A. Blue gives an example of a pilot and an airline flight attendant. He intimates their marital status, political views, financial status etc., were equal in worth. The difference was in their responsibilities. The work of the attendant is to keep the passengers comfortable thus keeping them content and favorable with the airlines. The pilot's job is to transport the passengers safely. Although the attendant's work, known as secondary leadership, is not seen as equally vital for keeping the passengers alive, but it is needed for keeping the business airlines alive.

The overall idea of secondary leadership is to be concerned for the benefit of those who are the recipients of the purpose of the service. Let's consider these assistants or secondary leaders from the Bible:

1. Silas to Paul
2. Aaron to Moses
3. Aquilla to Priscilla
4. Mark to Barnabas
5–7. Peter, James, and John to Jesus

Notable person, John the Baptist, and his attitude towards Jesus in St. John 1:29 (ESV),

> *"The next day John saw Jesus coming toward him*
> *and said Behold the lamb of God, who takes away*
> *the sin of the world."*

None of these secondary leaders, or assistants, were unhappy in their positions. They, like the primary leader, were mainly concerned for the people they ministered to. Both positions are necessary for the benefit of their constituents.

God calls and anoints certain people for the role of assistants (secondary leadership). It is a very important, appreciated and needed position. If that seems to be your assignment from God, walk in it, knowing that God is no respecter of persons and He's keeping a record of your devotion and dedicated commitment to His kingdom.

Be prepared to move forward in the plans that God has for you, and learn to be content Philippians 4:11b,

> *". . . for I have learned in whatsoever state that I am in,*
> *therewith to be content."*

However, be aware my sisters, contentment does not mean complacency Stay positioned for God to move you at His will and season in your life. Remember sisters, God knows who you are and where you are at all times and be assured what God has for you is for you. Don't allow discontentment to overwhelm you. Remain faithful to God and your call. Wait and listen for God and follow His directions.

ENVY

Sisters, we are to support and love one another, not judge, criticize or pull each other down by our attitudes towards each other. If your sister has been blessed to be called to pastor a church and you have not, support her. What God has for you is for you. Our mission is to be available for God to use us wherever He places us. You don't have to be in the spotlight for God to recognize your service. Throughout the Bible, we find it to be true that when God is in the plan, moreover when God gives you the plans there will be no failure. When God has blessed you, be thankful for what He's already blessed you with. Learn to be thankful and faithful to what God has given you. You fight envy by accepting what God can do with you and being faithful for what he has placed in your hands. Don't concern yourself with what others in the ministry have.

There is an account in the Bible in Psalm 73 regarding one of the chief musicians in the temple, his name is Asaph. It is the account of how he had spent a lot of time thinking about the prosperity of the wicked. More time than he should have spent. Then he came to himself and wrote what was his experience with this seemingly unfair situation. He shares in this Psalm how close he came to falling in the habit of envying the wicked and how they lived in prosperity. An example of that for us would be, a sister who has not been in the ministry as long as you, has now been called to pastor a well-established church, and you're still waiting. Sometimes there are moments when we ponder the events of our time, spending too much time thinking and worrying about what other people have. You must learn to appreciate God for the blessings He has given you. You are probably better off than you think—especially if you have a real relationship with God and trust in Him. Asaph, through all this worry did what God calls all His children to do and that is he kept his respect for God. He came to the true conclusion, deciding regardless of the apparent discrepancies in prosperity, he would follow and serve God. You will always benefit from God's Word and His Spirit. When you consider this, you don't have to envy anyone or be discontent but rather be grateful for the grace of God upon your life. The most important title that comes with the call is servant. Dedicate yourself to being the best servant you can be. Your fellow reverend sister's story is not your story. God is blessing you to have your own story.

PEOPLE PLEASING

Nothing can stunt your ministry more than people pleasing. People's opinion of you are just like "noses" as everyone has one. In the account of the seven churches addressed in the book of Revelation, the church at Laodicea was a "people pleasing" church. They bent over backwards to keep everyone happy. Christ referred to them as lukewarm in Revelation 3:16: *"So then because you are lukewarm and neither cold not hot, I will vomit you out of my mouth."* There is an old saying: "If you don't stand for something, you will fall for anything." You can't be all things to all people. You must stand for what is right in God's eyes.

I remember after my installation as pastor, one of the deacons made his way to the office to school me on how to succeed as their pastor. He proceeded to tell me how to handle certain people, how to handle certain situations, and how to approach my position as their pastor, what the church believed about Sunday school and Bible study participation, who would be best in certain positions, what the church needed and how to accomplish it according to what they had always done. On and on he went. In other words, according to him the only thing that I was to do was to preach and leave the rest of the decision making to the trustees.

I listened to him, attentively, thanked him respectfully (after all I had been raised by my parents to respect my elders), but I was compelled to answer him. I proceeded to inform him of the fact that my director was God. My intentions were to consult God first with my problems, rather than man like it suggests in 1Corinthians 2:5 (KJV),

"That your faith should not stand in the wisdom of men,
but in the power of God."

I shared with him that it was God who had placed me in the pastoral position and He would be the one who would direct me as to how to do the job He had placed me there to do. That is not to say that I would not consult with people in various situations for their opinions, but in reality, I would go to God first.

Needless to say, he did not receive my answer to his advice very well. However, he did realize I would not be a people pleaser and that I was fair in my dealings with the officers of the church. I would not be a "puppet" pastor in their hands.

Leading means listening to God. Learning to hear His voice above all others. In ministry, there will be many voices vying for your attention. Each one trying to convince you their advice is best.

It is imperative that we spend time with God to familiarize yourself with His voice.

Of course, you will not always be popular with everyone. If popularity is what you are desiring, you are setting yourself up for a fall. There will be decisions that you will have to make that will cause you to have to stand alone—but stand. Stand knowing that God is leading you.

Stand knowing that God will give you peace of mind during times of controversy.

II Timothy 3:12,

> *"Yea, and all that will live godly in*
> *Christ Jesus shall suffer persecution."*

Principle #2 from Dr. Charles Stanley's book, *Life Principles Bible* goes like this, "Obey God and leave all the consequences to Him." I find that when I follow this principle, I find it to be the best advice I could receive.

When we think of the life of Jesus, He was not very popular with the people in high places. Those who were in positions of earthly power, despised His humility, His honesty, His compassion for the lowly, and most of all, His ability to stand for what was right according to His Father. Jesus was not a "people pleaser." He did not sacrifice His faith in God for the approval of others. I would say to you my sisters, go and do likewise.

CONCLUSION

Whatever you do, don't allow discontent, envy or people pleasing to cause you to become "hung-up" in your purpose in ministry. Whatever your gift or placement in kingdom building may be, embrace it, and never doubt the importance of your ministry. An important example in the Bible is the Apostle Paul. He worked diligently planting churches according to the leading of The Spirit and God's plans and design. However, on several occasions after Paul had left the cities of the church plants, false teachers would creep in with the intention of tearing down what God had ordained

Paul to build up. But Paul did not allow this to overwhelm him. He did not allow the climate or prevailing influences of situations cause him to become disenchanted or discouraged in the ministry God had assigned to him. Sisters we must be just as diligent. Keep your relationship with God and your fellow sisters intact. God will provide everything that you need for this journey.

I Corinthians 2:9 (NKJV), "But as it is written:

"Eye has not seen, nor ear heard.
Nor have entered into the heart of man
The things which God has prepared for those who love Him."

Be encouraged, serve with love.

Chapter 7

BEING TESTED AND TEMPTED

In the everyday occurrences of life, there are intervals in this journey that call for us to trust God and God alone more fervently. Life teaches us every day. And as students and strangers in this land, we will ALL experience ups and downs, struggles as well as triumphs.

In school they teach us then they test us. God teaches us by testing us and the tests are always for our good. Every great person that God chose to use to further enhance the gospel was tested and tried either before or during their term of ministry. As we search the scriptures, we will not find anyone that had a "bed of roses" ministry. Some of the ones that God used mightily were tested to reveal their faith level to them were:

A. **John the Baptist:** when John had been arrested, from his prison cell he sent some of his disciples to ask Jesus if He was the Messiah or should they look for another. In Matthew 11:3-5, Jesus told them to go back and tell John the things they heard and seen. The blind see, the lame walk, the dead are raised, lepers are cleansed, etc.

B. **Elijah:** After he had shown Baal's prophets who the real God was, he had a moment of doubt. He thought he was the only real prophet left. Through many demonstrations of His power, God assured him that there were seven thousand who had not bowed their knee to Baal (I Kings 19:1-18).

C. **Peter:** denied knowing Christ. But after His resurrection, Jesus came to him and commissioned him to feed His sheep and lambs. Peter confessed his love and faith in Jesus more fervently (John 21:15-19).

D. **Paul:** Paul had his moment on the Damascus Road. As he was on his way to imprison the followers of Christ, Jesus met him and after an experience that was designed just for Paul, he was converted (Acts 9: 1-19).

E. **Moses:** When God commissioned him to go to Egypt and lead the Israelites to the Promised Land. Moses offered God excuses, however, God refused to accept them. Moses became a great prophet (Exodus 3:1-22).

F. **Abraham:** When God told him to sacrifice Isaac, his son of promise, God was testing his faith and obedience (Genesis 22:1-13).

In the book of Exodus 17:1-7, there is an account that occurred in a place called Rephidim. Rephidim was a place of testing for the Israelites as they journeyed on their way to the Promised Land. . The Israelites were as you know, God's chosen people. In Rephidim there was no water, just dry land. They were not in Rephidim by mistake in directions. They traveled as God led them. God had a purpose for leading them there. While at Rephidim, they questioned God and challenged Moses (see verses 2-3, 7). God showed them His power by having Moses to strike a rock to provide water for them.

This proved to them that God would take care of them no matter what they may encounter.

There may come a time in your life when you are faced with a situation (a Rephidim, if you will), You have prayed and done all you can do in your own strength and yet you find yourself with no relief in sight and you ask "God, don't you hear me?" It's not that you don't trust God's ability to help you, it's just that you are overwhelmed with your present need and the past interventions by God are being overshadowed by your present situation. Sometimes in life God will allow you to come face to face with situations that are seemingly impossible or at the very least painful to endure. It is times like these that God wants to demonstrate to you the magnitude of who He is, so that you will know, without a doubt, that God can do the impossible. God will let you know that He is present, and you can totally depend on Him during your greatest tests and difficulties. David wrote in Psalm 23:4,

> *"Yea, though I walk through the valley of the shadow of death,*
> *I will fear no evil; For you are with me;*
> *Your rod and Your staff, they comfort me."*

It's in the difficult places in your life that you will learn how resilient you are and how your faith in God is strengthened by each test. There is a song that has a line that says, ". . . the test only comes to make me strong." From James 1:2-4,

> *"My brethren, count it all joy when you fall into various trials,*
> *knowing that the testing of your faith produces patience.*
> *But let patience have its perfect work, that you may be*
> *perfect and complete, lacking nothing."*

You may be wondering how can you have joy in the midst of a trial/test? Joy comes in knowing that all tests come from God with an ending date. Also knowing that while you are going through your test, God is aware of where you are at all times, and He will not allow you to suffer beyond what you are able to bear.

You have to be strong enough in your personal commitment to the call of God on your life to face the challenges and test that comes with this journey. There will be times in your ministry when you will feel like giving up—but hang in there, God is your greatest supporter. There will also be times when you will have to take a stand all by yourself. Don't be discouraged, stand, knowing who you are standing for. Every test that you will go through will be a testimony regarding your experience as a woman of God.

Your testimony will encourage others to stay on the wall. In the book of Nehemiah (4:1-20) there is the account of him returning to Jerusalem to rebuild the wall. There were those who heard the wall was being rebuilt and tried to get Nehemiah to stop the work to meet with them (6:1-3). Nehemiah's response was" I am doing a great work, so that I cannot come down."

This was a test and Nehemiah had the best response and strength. You will have to be as strong in your commitment and pray for strength as he did to withstand the pressure Nehemiah was enduring (see v9c "Now therefore, O God strengthen my hands"). Satan's job is to try to depress you in your ministry, hoping that you will fall prey to the pressure and walk away from what God has called you to do.

The higher you go in your ministry and your service to God, the greater the challenges you will face. The more you antagonize, the devil is determined to try to cause you to doubt your call. This is when you will have to remember who placed you in this position. You will have to do as David did in I Samuel 30:1-6—" . . . encourage yourself in the Lord your God."

I Peter 3:14-17 says,

> *"But even if you should suffer for righteousness' sake, you are*
> *blessed. And do not be afraid of their threats nor be troubled.*
> *But sanctify the Lord God in your hearts, and always*
> *be ready to give a defense to everyone who asks you a*
> *reason for the hope that is in you, with meekness and fear;*
> *having a good conscience, that when they defame you as*
> *evildoers, those who revile your good conduct in Christ may be*
> *ashamed. For it is better, if it is the will of God, to suffer*
> *for doing good than for doing evil."*

BEING TEMPTED (TEMPTATION)

As leaders of God's people, we must pray to avoid falling into the snares of temptation. During your ministry you may find yourself being offered suggestions that seem okay or you may desire to attain certain things that on the surface doesn't appear that anyone could be adversely affected by your decision. You may have friends, associates or even family members who will present an attractive proposition to you, trying to convince you that "God knows your heart" and it's not really wrong. There is a scripture that you can refer to that will help to keep you on the right path, and it's found in Proverbs 14:12,

> *"There is a way that seems right unto man,*
> *but the end thereof are the ways of death."*

Be careful not to get caught up in trying to "keep up with the Joneses." Just because something seems to be working for a fellow sister in ministry does not mean it is part of God's plans for you. You'll find in James 1:14 this:

"But each is tempted when he is drawn away
by his own desires and enticed."

In Matthew 4:1-11 gives the account of the Holy Spirit leading Jesus into the wilderness to be tempted by the devil. After His baptism and recognition by God the Father, the devil tried to tempt Jesus psychologically, concerning pride and power. He will also try to tempt you with materialism and promised power. Sometimes in your desire for popularity you can be tempted to believe you have the power on your own, apart from God's plan and schedule for you, to become more significant in the public arena. Don't believe the lie.

Please be careful of those who promise to promote you. They will pump you up with promises that they have no power to fulfill. Keep in mind they have their stake in it, and in reality, it's all about them and their agenda.

Be cognizant of the ways of temptation entering into your spirit. We all have what is known as "gates." A gate is a way of entry. There are three gates

1. The eye gate—what you see
2. The ear gate—what you hear
3. The mouth gate—what you say:
   You will be most vulnerable when you have no support
   system, no one to look to for sound advice. You will
   always need that one person who you can trust to tell you
   the truth. That is why you will need a mentor and a prayer
   partner to turn to in times of temptation.

Of course, you should always go the word of God for the best advice: Hebrews 2:18,

"For in that He Himself has suffered, being tempted,
He is able to aid those who are tempted."

I Corinthians 10:13, it says,

> *"No temptation has overtaken you except such as is common to man: but God is faithful, who will not allow you to be tempted beyond what you are able, but with the temptation will also make the way of escape, that you may be able to bear it."*

There is a difference between testing and being tempted:

Tests: To prove by testing while under a trial to bring forth the good in us.
Tests come from God, and they are always for our good.

Temptation: comes by way of enticement or solicitation to evil.
Satan tempts us with the intention to make us fall.

When you call upon God for strength, courage, and patience, you are actually acknowledging the power of God to sustain you. You are telling God that you know He loves you and that He is an ever-present help in times of trouble. You are telling God that you honor Him, and that your faith in Him is strong, tried, and true. God is truly honored when we confess our dependence on Him. When we acknowledge He is omniscient, He is omnipresent, and He is omnipotent, God gets the glory. God already knows your strengths and the level of your faith. Your tests are designed to reveal to you the level of your strengths and weaknesses. It is through your tests, and temptations, that you will find your strengths and weaknesses.

The power of God will give you the strength to withstand any test an (or) temptation.

Stay strong, my sisters, because the journey is worth it all. Embrace and live by the truth of I John 4:4,

> *". . . because He who is in you is greater than he who is in the world."*

To God be the glory!

Chapter 8

DRESS FOR SUCCESS

In this society, how you dress says a lot about you. Some people are trend setters. When First Lady Michelle Obama bared her arms for the official White House portrait in 2008, it started a trend for women who were proud of their arms. We began to see more and more professional women baring their arms, particularly news reporters. Without trying, the First Lady had set a style that remains popular to this day. In the corporate world there is the conservative look of suits and stilettos for women and suits and ties for men. Lawyers are known for their style of dress. Carpenters, gardeners, doctors, nurses, mail carriers and soldiers all wear uniforms that identify their profession. As clergy, we wear our collars and robes.

As women in ministry there are some general guidelines that relate to us. Our dress code involves not only our physical appearance, but our emotional and spiritual wellbeing as well.

Physically: Beginning with our make-up, which should not be so dominant that it distracts from the message being preached. On the other side of the coin, we don't have to look "plain." A little make-up will improve the looks God has provided us with. Concerning our clothes and jewelry, please remember that in conventional pulpits those sitting behind us for the most part are males. They do not see our faces. It is appropriate to dress in clothes that flatter our physical appearance without calling attention to our back sides. We don't want to give our brothers any reason to cause their minds to "wander." Also consider the length of our skirts and dresses; when we sit down, they rise up. There are beautiful lap scarves for us to place on our laps. Remember we are primarily and exclusively promoting God. We are to also be modest in the choice of jewelry we wear when we are speaking. My first bit of knowledge came when my former pastor invited a female pastor to preach for our Annual Women's Day service. He assigned me to accompany her and take care of her needs.

When she arrived, she was wearing a beautiful pair of diamond earrings. As she changed into her robe, she took off the diamond earrings and replaced them with a smaller pair of pearl earrings. Out of curiosity, I asked why? She said the diamond earrings would be distractive. She did not want the congregation to pay attention to anything but the word. Needless to say, that was a lesson for me. Don't misunderstand—I am not suggesting that you don't wear diamond earrings when you preach, just be cognizant of the size and length of them. The same should be said for bracelets that make sounds every time you move your arm.

On one particular occasion, I was participating in a service where we were asked to wear our robes. It was an evening service and I had forgotten to remove a watch I had worn earlier that day when I had not been preaching. My daughter told me later that as I was performing my part in the service, that my watch was "cutting up." For those who don't know that vernacular, it means that my watch was calling attention to itself. Another lesson learned!

The attention should always be on the word of God, not on anything we may be wearing. We do well to remember to "keep it sophisticated and simple," the famous K.I.S.S. acronym. However, there is a group of young sisters that have been called to minister to "non-traditional" converts. These converts are not actively involved in churches that do not embrace their style of music and dress. They are more likely to follow a leader whose appearance closely resembles their free dress style, and they feel they can identify with. We all know that God is no respecter of persons, and He does not judge by outward appearance but rather offers salvation to all. Some ministers' assignment is to these "non-traditional" converts. The Apostle Paul shared with the church at Corinth (I Corinthians 9:19-23) that he did what was necessary that he *"might by all means save some."*

So, I say to you, my sister, if you have been called to such a ministry stay true to God and to yourself and do all things to the glory of God as you meet the needs of your congregation in word and dress style.

Additionally, it is imperative to take care of your body (See I Corinthians 6:19-20). With adequate rest, good nutrition and exercise you will have the strength and good health to carry-out the work God has called you to. Neglecting your body, not getting the proper rest will increase your chances of being ill, tiredness, exhaustion which would cause you to be unable to physically serve God the way I believe you desire to. Some people regard being exhausted as a banner of sacrifice. However, when you are not at your best, you cannot give your best. Learn to prioritize your schedule and take time for yourself for rest and relaxation.

Remember we only have this one body to use in service to God. Care for it properly and it will house the physical strength you will need for this journey. Even Jesus, in His humanness, took time to rest and sleep (see Matthew 8:23-24; Luke 8:22-23). I would say that taking care of your body is the first step in dressing for success.

Spiritually: In Ephesians 6, the Apostle Paul is declaring a style of dress for all Christians. It is not dressing on the outside but on the inside even though he describes it as armor. When you hear the word *armor*, you automatically think of war. In life there is warfare. In addition to the regular human calamities, we struggle with the operations of the powers of darkness as well as other enemies who would attempt to keep us from serving God. So, I believe it is safe to say that we are in a spiritual battle. The armor that the Apostle Paul is referring to is a general exhortation to being constant and consistent in our faith, encouraged in our daily walk, and prepared for Christian warfare. It is called the armor of God because He bestows it, but we are responsible for putting it on. Let's examine it:

The Girdle of Truth: (Verse 14) is mentioned first because it holds all the other armor together. This has reference to the doctrines of the truth of the Gospel. The truth is the word of God.

Psalm 119:89 says,

"Forever O Lord Thy word is settled in heaven."

Being girded about is a reference to a belt. Belts are used to secure our skirts or pants from falling down so we don't become exposed. In the same manner without the truth of God's Word we are exposed to doubt, fear, uncertainty, and misrepresentation of the truth of God's Word. The truth secures our faith which allows us to stand up in any situation.

John 8:32 says,

"And you shall know the truth,
and the truth shall make you free."

Knowing the truth keeps us strong in our resolve to follow Jesus at any cost. Without knowing the truth of God's Word, as a minister you have no security in your ministry. Knowing, believing and following the truth of God's Word will keep you grounded, sincere and committed to the ministry.

The Breastplate of Righteousness: (Verse 14b) It protects the heart. This righteousness of Christ is imputed to us in this breastplate.

Proverbs 4:23 reads,

> *"Keep thy heart with all diligence,*
> *for out of it are the issues of life."*

Your heart must be towards the people. In Matthew 12:34,

> *"Out of the abundance of the heart, the mouth speaks,"*

which means you will carefully choose words of kindness, compassion and love when speaking to and with people. Also, your words carry a great deal of weight and influence. People can be helped or hurt by what you say and how you say it. Psalm 119:11 says this,

> *"Your word I have hidden in my heart,*
> *That I might not sin against You."*

It would be very difficult to say the least to try to serve God and His people with sin lurking about in your heart and lifestyle. As ministers of the gospel, our prayer should always be Psalm 119:80 and that says,

> *"Let my heart be sound in your statues that I be not ashamed."*

The breastplate also represent the standards of God. It is no wonder that Satan wants to destroy our hearts—that is the seat of our Soul.

Feet Shod: (Verse 15) Signifies a prepared heart and mind to adhere to the Gospel, and abide in it, which then will enable us to walk with a steady pace in the ways of God in spite of the difficulties and dangers that may occur along the way. Some believe it also means to be prepared to spread the gospel of Jesus Christ. In either or both concepts, you must always be prepared. As a carrier of His Word, we never know when we will be called upon to teach and/or preach. I learned from my brother—remember he is a minister—to always have a message in your spirit that you can teach/preach at any time or at any place. May I suggest you select a passage of scripture that clearly represents your faith and speaks to your heart in a powerful way. For me it is Psalm 23.

I recall the first time I had to preach on a moment's notice. One Sunday morning about 7:30 a.m., I received a call from my then pastor's wife informing me that he had laryngitis and was unable to speak. He needed me to preach the 11:00 a.m. Service. Fortunately, I had followed my brother's advice and was able to teach from Psalm 23 with a three-and-a-half-hour notice.

The message of the Gospel offers the promise and possibility of peace. Taking the message of peace to the world is the main purpose of your call. Being prepared is the foundation of your ministry. The Apostle Paul's advice to Timothy in II Timothy 4:2,

> *"Preach the Word!*
> *"Preach the Word; be ready in season and out of season.*
> *Convince, rebuke, exhort, with all long-suffering and teaching."*

Having your feet shod, refers to putting shoes on your feet with the idea of moving about. Remember–prepare yourself with His Word and go!

The Shield of Faith: (Verse 16) Faith in Christ is our universal shield of defense. It's what we use against those fiery darts of the devil. The word of God says that we are to walk by faith. When we think about a shield, we automatically think about security and safety. When used properly it protects us in any direction that we turn. The shield of faith infers that we can be secured and safe as our faith places us in God's hands. Your faith in God will carry you in your ministry. It will protect you during time of trials that you may encounter. It will protect you from the fiery darts of slander against your good name, jealousy, lies, criticism, words of doubt spoken about you and your ministry etc., that will come at you. Ask God to put His shield of protection around you. It will give you the strength to stand up confidently against those fiery darts of the devil. Your shield of faith in God is a necessity in ministry. For more on faith see the chapter entitled 'Faith Check.'

The Helmet of Salvation: (Verse 17a) The helmet protects the head where our knowledge of God and His unfailing love is stored. Salvation must be our helmet, which is hope, trust in God and assurance of God's love. The Apostle Paul writes in I Thessalonians 5:8 (KJV),

"But let us who are of the day, be sober,
putting on the breastplate of faith and love;
and for a helmet, the hope of salvation."

Always know that your salvation is sure. Ephesians 1:13-14 (KJV),

". . . the gospel of your salvation: in whom also after that ye
believed, ye were sealed with that holy Spirit of promise, which
is the earnest of our inheritance until the redemption of the
purchased possession, unto the praise of his glory."

Your salvation is a gift from God as stated in Ephesians 2:8 (KJV),

"For by grace you have been saved through faith,
and that not of yourselves; it is the gift of God."

Walk in the assurance of your salvation.

The Sword of the Spirit: (Verse 17b) It is the Word of God. Which is imperative in the life of all Christians. It is in the Bible where we find strength for daily living, hope for our future, and faith in God and His love to carry us through. Christ used the word of God to defeat the devil during His time of temptation as referenced in Matthew 4:1-10.

The petition for prayer is stated in Verse 18. Prayer, which we dedicated a chapter to, is also in our arsenal of armor that we are to dress in every day. This armor constitutes the spiritual armor of dress for your protection from the daily challenges you will face in your ministry.

The complete outfit of all the armor is faith, love commitment, protection, safety, and confidence. Be sure to dress yourself in this spiritual armor every day.

Emotionally: In addition to the armor of God, we are to dress daily in the peace of mind found in (Philippians 4:8-9). However, there are some character traits/ emotions that we are to never include in our wardrobe:

1. Unforgiveness: Breaks your fellowship with God (see Matthew 6:14; Mark 11:25).
2. Impatience: (Ecclesiastes 7:8)
3. Discontent: (Job 15:11-13; Ecclesiastes 6:9)
4. Anger: (Psalm 37:8, Ecclesiastes 7:9, and James 1:19)
5. Pride: (Deuteronomy 8:17, I Corinthians 10:12, Galatians 6:3, and I Samuel 2:3)
6. Jealousy: (Romans 13:13; James 3:16)
7. Envy: (Galatians 5:26)
8. Overall Bad Attitude: You cannot have a right relationship with God engaging in ungodly emotions and actions (Ephesians 4:18).

Sisters, we are to be beautiful daughters of God. I have been fortunate to attend a conference for women in ministry. The conveyer is a beautiful woman physically. Her personality and the way she interacted with the conference attendees made her even more beautiful. The ministers and pastors that completed the conference roster were also beautiful women who were dressed beautifully and fashionably and yet there were no distractions from the word of God. They were all women of integrity which was evident in their demeanor and the content of their messages. This shows we don't have to appear masculine or dress inappropriately as women of God. The real beauty comes from the inside; they include humility, confidence, commitment and love for God and His people. Your appearance, integrity and attitude should complement each other. You will not be properly dressed to present the word of God if you don't exhibit all of these. That's what people should see and remember about us along with the word of God that we have been called to preach. That is how as ministers of God, daughters in particular, we should all dress.

Chapter 9

PASTORS / A WORD TO MY SISTER-PASTORS

I will pray for you. I will pray for your strength in the Lord. The journey you are on, I've been there. Without knowing you personally, I am sure we share some commonalities simply because we are leaders. We lead people who have different agendas, personalities, and character traits.

I take time to write specifically to you sharing from my experience some pastoral encouragement and also suggestions relating to your role as a leader, wife, mother, sibling, and relative.

AS PASTOR /SERVANT LEADER

First of all, remember this journey and call are about God—not you. Keep that fact at the forefront of your pastorate. Remember, God has chosen you. He chose you for this stewardship and He trusted you with His most important creation—His people. Also remember the people belong to God—not you. God has placed them in your care. Lead them with the same love and care that a good shepherd would their sheep.

In John 10:14 Jesus says,

> *"I am the good shepherd; and I know*
> *My sheep and am known by My own."*

You have been entrusted by God Himself to also be a good shepherd. Pray always for God's guidance, even for what you consider to be simple things. In Song of Solomon 2:15a,

> *"The little foxes that spoil the vines."*

In other words, give attention to the small things, too. 1 Corinthians 15:58 (NJKV),

> *"Therefore, my beloved brethren, be steadfast, immovable,*
> *always abounding in the work of the Lord,*
> *knowing that your labor is not in vain in the Lord."*

I offer these words of encouragement to all servant leaders. It is refreshing to know that we must realize that we are first of all "servants." It does not matter what our title is, it is to our advantage to see ourselves as God's servants. However, there must always be a foundation first. A foundation that all servant leaders must build upon.

I'll share with you one of my favorite leaders in the Bible. He is not often preached about as much as David, Moses, or Paul. But in his book, you will find the necessary components for a good foundation for leaders—the book of Nehemiah. Some of the foundational principles found in his book are:

I. **You must love the Lord and His people:** In Nehemiah 1:1-6, we see he is praying for God's help regarding his fellow Jewish people in Jerusalem. Pastors must have the heart of God and be concerned about the needs of their congregation—personal, emotional, and spiritual needs.

II. **You must have a strong faith in God:** Nehemiah fasted and prayed. God heard his heart and his desire and answered his prayer. (Nehemiah 2:1-8) You must go before the Lord knowing that He will hear and answer your prayers. You must be confident that God will supply everything that you need for your success as his servant leader.

III. **You must rely on God for directions:** In Nehemiah 2:11-16, when Nehemiah arrived in Jerusalem, he acted according to God's directions. You won't need the opinions of a group. Spend quiet time alone with God to assess the needs and you will hear from God on how you are to handle situations. Please don't misunderstand this principle. You need reliable people you can count on. No one is an island. When you get your directions from God, He will lead you to, or send you the right people to support you, the people that don't have a problem recognizing you as the leader, that don't mind following your directions and vision, the ones who won't try to compete with you or challenge your intellect. Trust God to place people in your life who will encourage you, pray for you and support you.

IV. **Leaders must be aware:** Be aware that all of your enemies are not on the outside of your congregation

(See Nehemiah 6:10-13). Sometimes those that you trust can be influenced by the enemy and will ultimately be persuaded to betray or discourage you. It is times like that when you rely on God for insight, intuition, and strength.

The foundation of your ministry is built upon these and other valuable principles that will keep you strong in the Lord. There will be times when you feel like Moses at Rephidim (Exodus17:4) when he asked God, "What shall I do with these people?" However, your faith in God will propel you, constrain you, and keep you moving ahead knowing that the journey you're on is one of honor and sacrifice. I heard Bishop T.D. Jakes say, "Once you are in a leadership position, you're telling God that you are willing to be sacrificed." Take comfort in knowing that God has promised to be with you, and as long as you are obedient to Him, He will keep you standing strong.

Keep in mind, the church belongs to God—not you. He has not handed it over to you; after all it is considered to be the "Bride of Christ." By church I am not referring to a building structure. I am aware that some pastors take ownership of buildings, but the real church- God's people— belong to Him.

As a pastor, I was always in awe of the fact that God entrusted me to lead His people. Often, I would tell people it was not that I was so special. God could have taken an unsavory person from the streets, cleaned her up and gave her the same grace that He gave to me. That's how awesome our God is. That fact kept me grounded and it kept me from becoming too prideful. I never lost sight of the fact that God chose me out of the abundance of His divine will .The position as a pastor was my destiny, determined by God before I was born. That keeps me forever humble and indebted to God. Keep God first in all that you do.

FAMILY

If you are married, keep the role as pastor and wife in the correct order. If you are your husband's pastor, leave her at the church and be his wife at home. Your husband is the head of the household and your calling to the pastorate has not changed that. Men are natural protectors, and they like to feel needed. You may be a pastor, or minister, but in his eyes you are his beloved, his wife, whom he promised in the marriage vows to love and protect, don't reverse the role.

If he is not on the same level as you are spiritually, be patient, pray for him. It is not your job to convert him or harass him regarding his personal relationship with God. God will deal with him in God's own way and time. I Peter 3:1-2 says,

> *"Wives, likewise, be submissive to your own husbands, that*
> *even if some do not obey the word, they, without a word,*
> *may be won by the conduct of their wives when they observe*
> *your chaste conduct accompanied by fear."*

Because you have authority at the church, it does not transfer to your home. I was also my husband's pastor. But the moment we got into our car to drive home; the role was reversed. My role then was his wife, not his pastor, which was the correct order. Be a God ordained wife, it will make a difference in your marriage and family.

If you are your children's, grandchildren's, and siblings' pastor, the same applies at home and family gatherings. Take off your pastor hat and be "Mom," Grandmother," and/or "sister." Enjoy your family as a loving, caring family member. Your family does not need you as their pastor at home. They need you to be the person you are in relation to them.

When you are invited to family gatherings or social events, your presence should elicit joy and not disdain. If your spirit feels uncomfortable around those who are consuming liquid spirits, do your due diligence by saying your hellos, give hugs and kisses stay for a while and make an early departure. If while you are there you are asked biblical questions, answer them briefly with a promise of future time together to get deeper into the topic being questioned. You don't need to show up with a large Bible with the intention of preaching and saving those you feel need to be saved. When Jesus attended the wedding at Cana of Galilee, He went as a guest, (see John 2:1-2). It was only after His mother approached Him that He acted in His Messianic role (see John 2:3-10).

Jesus met people where they were. As a result, he was accused of associating with sinners. He was being a loving, caring, concerned friend to the people. Even though He was always fully God as well as being fully man, He never lauded His Kingship over people. Jesus displayed perfect character which allowed people to feel comfortable in His presence.

Jesus kept it real and so should you.

PERSONAL

Always keep for yourself a shoulder to cry on. I am aware of praying to God, letting Him be your burden bearer. However, sometimes you just need a human being to connect with here on earth. For me that was my brother, and a fellow pastor friend. With my brother I could share personal hurts and concerns. He would always take time to listen to me without criticizing or judging me. But he was always fair in his assessment of any situation I shared with him. He would tell me honestly if I was the culprit. Most importantly, he always prayed for me and with me.

My pastor friend and I would get together over breakfast or lunch frequently and share *church* concerns. She and I would encourage and motivate each other to keep moving forward and trusting God in spite of the difficulties we faced. We would inevitably end our time together talking about the goodness of God and praying for each other's strength and perseverance.

Always strive to show warmth and compassion wherever you go. Whatever you do, never display a "superior" attitude at any time or place. You never know who is watching you. Your attitude could be the catalyst that bring people to the desire to get to know the God you have been called to share with the world. On the flip side, a bad display of character could be a "turn off" for those who have not yet said yes to God.

When you are invited as a guest speaker, before you arrive at the church extending the invitation, make it your business to find out the overall custom of that particular congregation. Believe it or not, churches have personalities. What may be accepted at one church may not be accepted at another. Some churches flow freely in the Spirit of God, others can be very reserved. Also be careful with your linguistic style, considering the age of the congregants.

LEADERSHIP

As leaders, pastors in particular, we have the awesome responsibility to be encouragers and peacemakers. As we are led of the Lord let us lead others to the one person who has the ability to provide them eternal life.

Always be ready and available for God and allow Him to lead you. Be content to do whatever He desires you to do, wherever He sends you to do it, and however He decides to use the gift. Keep in mind, He called you, He placed the gift in you to serve Him in the capacity He desires. Your job is to follow His lead and He will not disappoint you.

"Made In His Image" has to be more than words for us. When we embrace the fullness of this statement our lifestyle will be fruitful for the Kingdom.

To God be the glory!

Chapter 10

FAITH CHECK

Every believer is familiar with the description of faith found in Hebrews 11:1(NJKV),

"Now faith is the substance of things hoped for,
the evidence of things not seen."

There are two key words in this passage: substance: a fundamental or characteristic part or quality; and hope: a desire accompanied by expectation of or belief in fulfillment. We all embrace the essence of this scripture as part of our faith walk.

Webster defines faith as: complete confidence, firm belief in something for which there is no proof. We all know that Jesus Christ is the foundation and root of our faith. In Hebrews 11:6, it says, *"Without faith it is impossible to please him."*

Faith is an action word, and we operate in faith every day. By faith, we believe our car will start when we place the key in the ignition and turn it or push a button with the newer models. By faith, we work on a job for two weeks before receiving a paycheck. By faith, we eat food that we don't personally prepare not knowing the safety precautions taken by the manufacturer to ensure it won't harm us.

However, personal faith that is needed to sustain you spiritually, mentally, and sometimes physically, is not a reality in your life until it's been exercised. You will never know your true level of faith until you've tested it in some situation that for the most part you did not choose.

The disciples did not know how little their faith was until a storm arose while they were out on the sea, and they began to panic (see Matthew 8:23-26.)

Believe me, my sister, your road is paved with faith. Faith in God that you must know personally in order to trust His promises to never leave or forsake you, to be that ever-present help, to be the lifter of your head; the God who orders your steps, give you joy unspeakable and peace that surpasses understanding. To know God is to totally trust Him, and that is where your faith takes off from.

It is the one thing that we can be in control of.. We may not be the pilot of our fate, but we most definitely are the pilots of our faith. No one but you and I can operate our faith.

Our responsibility is to walk in faith every day. However, there are times when we need a faith check. We can always re-visit some basic facts and principles that will help us in our quest to assure ourselves that we are sure our faith in God has not wavered. There are at least three things to keep in mind as we begin our "Faith Check:"

1. God always responds to fervent prayer.
2. Standing firm on your faith in God is imperative.
3. Faith, prayer, and praise brings positive results.

FAITH AND PRAYER

In our lifetime, there will be times when battles come into our life. A battle can be anything that disrupts our sense of security, our peace of mind, or produces a negative effect. You realize you have no immediate answer, and you are not able to meet the challenge successfully in your own strength. You realize that your only alternative is to go to God in prayer and pray in faith believing, knowing God will come to your rescue.

Once you have prayed in faith, you have to release all anxiety and fear. You cannot trust God and worry at the same time. You must wait in faith knowing God has heard and is answering your prayer. Keep in mind, God knows where you are and what's going on in your life at all times. It is important that you understand you won't always experience the manifestation of your prayer right away.

In the book of Habakkuk, he had some concerns about the treatment of the poor by the leaders in Judah. He prayed to God for an answer. The answer he received was not what he expected. He learned from God that he would have to *wait* for the manifestation of the answer he was given.

Keep in mind God does not always answer our prayers in the manner and time we want them to be answered. But our faith in God reassures us that in His own time and way, He will answer our prayers. Habakkuk's faith in God assured him that whatever God chose to do would be to their benefit. His response, found in Habakkuk 3:17-18 (NKJV) says,

> *"Though the fig tree may not blossom, Nor fruit be on the vines; Though the labor of the olive may fail, And the fields yield no food; Though the flock may be cut off from the fold, And there be no herd in the stalls—Yet will I rejoice in the Lord, I will joy in the God of my salvation."*

He exercised unwavering faith in God.

Your faith in God will be your weapon against fear and doubt when you pray. During your ministry don't get weighed down with things that you cannot control or may not even understand. Just pray in faith, trusting God, He will always come through for you.

Matthew Henry writes "An active faith can give thanks for a promise though it be not yet performed. Knowing that God's bonds are as good as ready money." Praying in faith and giving God thanks encourages your heart towards God. Prayer is the catalyst that will catapult your faith to the level of complete faith in God and His love for you.

STAND FIRM ON YOUR FAITH

You have to take a firm stand on your faith in God's power, providence, and promises.

Your entire salvation is based on your faith in God, His grace, and His Word. Romans 10:9-10 reads this way,

> "If you confess with your mouth the Lord Jesus and believe in
> your heart that God raised Him from the dead, you will be
> saved, For with the heart one believes unto righteousness, and
> with the mouth confession is made unto salvation."

Standing firm on your faith will sometimes cause people to question your actions. In Genesis 6, God commissioned Noah to build an ark. No doubt the people questioned him about what he was doing. (This statement is my personal opinion; it is not written in the account of Noah and the ark. However, considering human nature it is not unreasonable to believe Noah was questioned and perhaps even ridiculed for what he was doing). However, he did not allow anything or anyone to hinder him in his quest to do what God had commissioned him to do. He stood firm on his faith in God and completed his project. We all know the end results of his faith (See Genesis 6:8-8:19).

There are many instances in the Bible where Jesus accredited people's faith to receiving their blessings. Beginning in the Old Testament with Abraham and his willingness to offer his son Isaac as a sacrifice (see Genesis 22).

In the New Testament, the servant of the centurion was ill (Matthew 8:5-13) and the Gentile woman whose daughter was possessed with an evil spirit (Matthew 15.21-28) are but two examples of strong faith resulting in blessings.

Standing firm on your faith in God will impel you to wait and expect a blessing. While you are standing firm on your faith God is keeping you day by day, proving that His grace is sufficient.

FAITH, PRAYER, AND PRAISE

In II Chronicles 20, we find Jehoshaphat faced with the news of the impending attack of three opposing nations coming against him. On hearing the news, Jehoshaphat "set himself to seek the Lord, and proclaimed a fast throughout all Judah" (verses 3-12). He prayed God's promises back to Him. He had no great army, but he had great faith in God to deliver him because of God's promises. God sent word to him that the battle was not his but God's (verse 15). In addition to fasting and praying, Jehoshaphat organized a praise team to go before them to declare the goodness of God (verse 21). Jehoshaphat won this battle with faith, prayer, and praise. Marvin Sapp recorded a song entitled "Teach My Hands to War," implying that when we praise, our enemies will have to vacate our space. Praise is an extension of your faith in the God you trust.

This is an excellent example for all believers; don't allow your circumstances to interfere with or minimize your faith. Hebrews 11:6b reads,

> *"For he that cometh to God must believe that He is, and that*
> *He is a rewarder of those that diligently seek Him."*

Faith can be exercised by your prayer and praise even during difficult times.

While you are waiting for the change to come continue to pray, praise, and believe. Psalm 50:15 declares,

> *"Call upon Me in the day of trouble;*
> *I will deliver you, and you shall glorify Me."*

Also consider Psalm 34:1 (KJV),

> *"I will bless the Lord at all times;*
> *His praise shall continually be in my mouth."*

In addition to those three areas of faith, there are other components to be considered during your "faith check."

FAITH WHEN YOUR BELIEFS ARE CHALLENGED

During times of difficulties regarding your belief, you may sometimes have to fight for your faith.

You won't have to physically fight for your faith, but you will have to keep your mind filled with the love of God to prevent Satan from invading your mind and planting seeds of doubt. One of Satan's tactics is to infiltrate your mind with doubt, attempting to influence you not to believe God. Satan will catch you at your weakest moments because he knows as long as he can fill your mind with doubt and fear, you will not completely trust God.

Sadly, Satan is not the only source of doubtful influence you will encounter. People that you listen to can also feed doubt into your spirit. That's why my sister, you must be very careful who you allow into your personal space and your sphere of influence. Don't allow negative influence to cause you to question your faith in God. Sometimes you will have to lovingly disagree with others and stand firm on what you know and believe. At times like these, you will have to fight for your faith by pushing those negative thoughts and opinions out of your mind and pray. The God in you gives you the power to fight for your faith.

Also, keep the Word of God alive in your life. Read your Bible for strength. God's Word is filled with words of comfort, strength and of course love. Your faith is increased through the Word of God. Having knowledge of God and having faith in Him are the anchors that will keep you above waters. Stand firm and watch God work in your favor when your faith is being challenged.

RADICAL FAITH

Webster's definition of radical is: disposed to make extreme changes in existing views, habits, conditions, or institutions.

Radical faith is when you have no clue how Jesus is going to answer your prayer or act on your behalf. You just *know* He will. A perfect example of radical faith is the account of the woman with the issue of blood. Because of Levitical laws on uncleanliness, with her condition, she was not allowed to be in a crowd. I believe this woman was sick and tired of being sick and tired, so she encouraged herself to act. This woman followed her spirit and moved out on "radical faith." She made her way through the crowd and touched the hem of Jesus' garment. Her faith was not in the robe but in her action. The minute she began making her way to Jesus, her healing was a guaranteed blessing. Jesus said her faith had made her whole. Her radical faith evoked a commendation from Jesus that is permanently recorded in the Bible (see Matthew 9:20-22, Mark 5:25-34, and Luke 8: 43-48).

Because you and I know the power of faith and the provisions of God you somehow move beyond your ordinary faith. You step outside of the box and move into an illogical way of believing that God has already granted you favor. You have to walk like you believe, talk like you believe, act like you believe. Call those things that are not as though they were. When deciding to exercise your radical faith, don't share your plans with anyone else. Most people will not understand you or your faith. Radical faith has no logic and remember, sometimes your faith looks foolish to others. Some situations call for radical faith.

ACTIVE/VISIBLE FAITH THAT WILL BENEFIT THE KINGDOM

In Mark 2, we find the account of four men actively demonstrating their faith in Jesus. Evidently these four men had heard Jesus preach before and possibly had witnessed His miraculous works. Their faith in Jesus compelled them to do what they did. For them to take the chance of destroying someone's property to get their friend to Jesus was an act of strong faith in action. The faith demonstrated by these men, is an example of visible faith in Jesus. Verse five states, "When Jesus saw their faith . . ." When people are able to see or witness our faith, it speaks positively for the kingdom of God.

UNWAVERING FAITH

Mark 11:22 is one of the most profound statements in the Bible where Jesus says to them,

". . . have faith in God."

In the context of this statement the reference is to miraculous faith. However, this statement—have faith in God—is inclusive and it applies to every area of faith. Whatever the situation to have faith in God is the ultimate answer.

You must have faith to believe that what God has promised to do He will do. Faith in His love for you, that by the way, He has already proven it at Calvary. That demonstration of love keeps us rooted and grounded in faith in God. Faith in His providing for you, scripture says that He knows our needs. Faith that He will supply all of our need according to His riches in glory in, Christ Jesus. Faith that a relationship with Him will not leave you empty but will fill you to the brim with what you need and desire. Faith that He will be with you when you go through the trials of life. God will test you by Your faith, but He will measure you by your obedience.

The Apostle Peter demonstrated faith in Jesus when he stepped out of the boat and actually walked on water (Matthew 14:29). It wasn't until he took his eyes off Jesus that he began to sink. His faith wavered when he began to focus on his surroundings. Unwavering faith is focused on God—not on your strength (or someone else's) or your circumstances/ surroundings.

Of course, there will be times when you will have to trust others, but your unwavering faith is in God and how he will work in them to do what you are trusting them to do.

One thing is sure, you can't learn faith by reading about it in a book. You will need to go beyond the intellectual aspect of faith to the actuality of experiencing the reality of faith personally.

There were many times during my pastorate when all I had was my faith in God. On a personal level, my faith in God carried me through various health issues including a cancer scare; marital issues and times when I felt very much alone dealing with burdens that I could not share with anyone. But my faith in God carried me through ALL the difficult times in my life. Even a chapter in my life that I am dealing with currently, my faith keeps me standing strong. That's why I can assure you that God knows where you are and what's going on in your life at all times.

My sister, faith in God is one of the greatest assets you will ever have in this lifetime. It's also one of the most needed. So, I say to you make full use of your faith in God and enjoy the benefits of blessings that your faith will bring you. Hold firmly to your faith in Him; He will never let you down.

Remember this: Worry looks back but faith looks up!

Chapter 11

PREACH THE WORD

As we watch the news, the majority of what we see and hear is not good news. Jobs lost due to downsizing, or the company is moving to another state where the taxes are not sky high. Foreclosures because people are not able to pay their mortgage.

Food scares, salmonella and other life-threatening bacteria in our food Police shootings and other family tragedies in our society.

Home invasions, robberies, rogue police departments and officers.

If there ever was a time when we needed some good news, now is the time. A songwriter once wrote, "If we ever needed the Lord, we sure do need Him now." There is a place designed to do just that. The church was created by God as a place for the saints as well as the unsaved to come and hear the good news of Jesus Christ.

Every Sunday across America, people gather in their respective churches to hear a message from the Lord via their preacher. Most have not necessarily taken the time during the week to study their Bibles, attend Bible study, or small groups where the word of the Lord is being taught. Unfortunately, there are not many messages being preached about the holiness of God. So, the people come with the expectation they will get a message that will satisfy them in their particular lifestyle. They trust their pastor who they feel have a special connection with God, therefore whatever the pastor says they accept as the truth, the whole truth and nothing but the truth. Some pastors are all too happy to deliver a diverse content in their messages today to please their congregation. Some sermons can be classified as:

SOCIAL SERMONS

In the context of "social sermons" messages are preached that feed the congregation what they want to hear, rather than what they need to hear. For example, if there is a large number of single women in the congregation, there will be messages referring to how to find the perfect mate, and maybe a reference or two on how God can help you while you are waiting for "Mr. Right." Much of the message has no scriptural support. Depending on the charisma of the pastor, congregations pay generously to hear messages that feed their egos and feelings.

What must be preached and to whom:

THE POST-MODERN GENERATION

Sadly, many of our younger generation are expecting to hear something new or what they refer to as "contemporary." Millennials and GenZs are searching for something. Unfortunately, many feel it's in materialism and what they are able to gain for themselves. They don't understand there is "nothing new under the sun" (Ecclesiastes 1:9b) and most importantly they must understand that the word of God does not change and there are no new revelations to pacify their generation.

However, there are those who are truly seeking to know God. They are in pursuit of the true knowledge of God, and how it can be applied to their lives. They are part of a technological age which gives them access to find information that may not be as theologically sound or correct. This is where you will need to be prepared to share the truth with them. Which of course means that you will need to be diligent, persistent, and consistent in the ways of becoming knowledgeable in the word of God. I Timothy 2:15 (NKJV) it says,

> *"Be diligent to present yourself approved to God,*
> *a worker who does not need to be ashamed,*
> *rightly dividing the word of truth."*

The key words are "rightly dividing," as this group of truth seekers have seen their parents and perhaps even grandparents live religious lives. They are seeking for the keys to effective and honorable Christian living, which is more than just being religious or appearing to be.

One of the most important areas with them is the area of persuasion by communication and ethics. Meaning you sister preacher, must live your life on the top level. The days are long past when preachers are given passes in their character simply because they are preachers. Good character is the foundation for persuading people to follow the word you are striving to convince people is God ordained. They need to see your faith in God and the word of God being actualized in your lifestyle.

The days are over when pastors and preachers can just preach and assume they won't be challenged by people who need more clarification on certain Bible passages. As preachers and teachers use the Bible to answer questions, they had better be ready to discuss intelligently and lovingly the context of the scriptures, not just putting out shallow answers.

LIBERAL AND MATERIAL SEEKERS

There are some people who will follow you according to the word you preach. The more you tell them about personal material gain, the larger following you will have. There will be some who will want to hear about a Jesus who will adjust Himself according to their way of life. A Jesus who will look the other way when they are not living according to His Word. They want a Jesus who is a compromising liberal, one who will throw morals and ethics out the proverbial "window" if they show up at church every once in a while, claiming to be followers of Jesus.

Through no fault of their own, many have had God presented to them in such a way that misinforms them about forgiveness. Your responsibility is to teach the truth about forgiveness. God is truly a forgiving God. However, there is a condition on their part. Teach them to embrace the truth of 1 John 1:9 (KJV) which says,

> *"If we confess our sins, He is faithful and just to forgive us our sins and to cleanse us from all unrighteousness."*

THE MISINFORMED

There will be those who will come to hear you preach and teach and will be challenged by the truth that you preach. Many have been exposed to bad gospel and cultic teachings. Your job is to first of all be patient with them. You must realize it is sometimes difficult to unlearn something that has been taught to them all of their life. But as you expose them to the truth of God's Word, remember, in Isaiah 55:11, the verse reads like this:

> *"So shall My word be that goes forth from My mouth; It shall not return to Me void, But it shall accomplish what I please, And it shall prosper in the thing for which I sent it."*

When the truth of God's Word is heard by a heart that is open to know the truth, God will make the change in their hearts.

My first experience in this area came when a young man who had been studying with another religion, became a member of the Sunday school class that I taught. He totally misunderstood John 14:12 which says,

> *"Most assuredly, I say to you, he who believes in Me,*
> *the works that I do he will do also; and greater works*
> *than these he will do, because I go to my Father."*

He had been taught that we would do more and better miracles than Jesus had done, setting ourselves up to be more powerful than Jesus. It took some time and patience on my part teaching him that greater had reference to **quantity** rather than **quality**; Jesus did His works in three short years. We normally will have more time than just three years to do kingdom work.

ENCOURAGE FAITH

For those who identify themselves as believers, share with them that things won't always go the way they plan. Even believers will face difficult times in their lives. Encourage them to hold onto their faith and trust in God which will enable them to go through any trial successfully. When they know and trust God, they will better understand that no matter what storm or difficulty they may face, God can give them rest and peace in the middle of it. Faith in God, trust in His Word, must be preached over and over again.

PROBLEMATIC AREAS

Within the membership of the average church, we have members who are struggling with their sexuality. We must be very careful how we teach and preach about sexuality. Because the Spirit of God uses teaching and preaching to change lives, we must use the truth of the scriptures to teach what God says regarding this very difficult topic. Human sexuality is a very emotional subject. We must understand that we are talking about human beings, with the same feelings and emotions that all God's people have. We must be considerate, not judgmental, on how we respond to all types of situations, particularly in the area of homosexuality. Again, when dealing with a subject as sensitive as this, the main focus is to teach that God can make a difference in their lives. However, we must teach the truth without being apologetic. We are to stand with our brothers and sisters who are struggling with homosexuality, but we must also stand firm on the word of God.

DELIVERY OF THE WORD

Please teach the Bible with kindness, remembering there was a time when you had to be taught to trust God. You must not preach in a judgmental, dogmatic style. Your job is to offer healing and hope. You must not use the preaching forum as a soapbox to air out your feelings and opinions. You must remember that trusting and believing in God is a process and it doesn't happen overnight. The time that you spend in explaining the truth in love will also demonstrate the love and patience of God that He has for all of us. It is the Word that saves, not you. Your job is just to preach and teach the truth from a Bible that has not been translated to the extent that the true essence of God's purpose is not being presented.

Woman of God, always ask God for wisdom before you preach. In 1 Chronicles 2:10 even Solomon, known for his wisdom, prayed to God:

> *"Now give me wisdom and knowledge, that I may go out and come in before this people."*

Remember, this word that you preach is designed to implement positive change in the lives of the hearers. Only the wisdom of God can accomplish that.

Please realize that the only person you have to please is God. Never compromise God's Word to gain popularity or members.

The main focus is to preach the Cross, the Blood, Jesus, salvation and the high cost of sin. Somehow, we have lost the main focus in our churches. There is too much "social gospel" being preached. The true message of the gospel must be preached. You, my sister must raise the banner of Christ and the Cross and invite people to come under it for their salvation. You have been given the awesome responsibility to teach and preach the word of God, you dare not mismanage the trust that God has placed in you.

It is imperative that we preach messages of truth and hope. We must preach messages about the goodness of God, how He will bear our burdens, heal our bodies, provide for the necessities of life, and His faithfulness to His Word. However, we must not preach this message of God in such a fashion that it be misunderstood, misinterpreted, or misleading, to the degree that many people only serve God for what they can get from Him. It is as if they are playing "let's make a deal" with God. God wants a relationship with us and His promises are available to all who obey His commands. We cannot continue to portray God as someone we can buy blessings from. God is good, and we can depend on Him for our needs. Paul writes in Philippians 4:19 (KJV), "But my God shall supply all your need," in the midst of churching and religion, the true essence of God diffuses our greed and desires.

We must return to preaching messages about the holiness of God. In Isaiah 6, Isaiah was in awe of the holiness of God. In a time when moral and spiritual decay had peaked in Judah, it was important for Isaiah to see God in His holiness. Holiness means morally perfect, pure, and set apart from all sin. In the vision that Isaiah saw, he witnessed the glory of God. He saw the Sovereignty of God; he saw God as King. He saw the power of God, the Lord of hosts. He saw the dominion of God, Adonai, the Lord Jesus Christ. Isaiah saw God high and lifted up, sitting on a throne of:

A. Glory—before which we must all worship.
B. Government—under which we must be subject as He is our eternal judge.
C. Grace—to which we have been invited to come boldly.

His throne is high and lifted up above all competition and contradiction. God is clothed with honor and majesty. Scripture says that His train filled His temple. There were angels, the attendants celebrating the His glory and holiness. They said, "Holy, holy, holy" for God is infinitely holy, originally holy, and perfectly holy. Or possibly one holy for the Father, one holy for the Son and one holy for the Spirit, for these three are one. Each angel had six wings; two covered their face, because they were unworthy to look on the holy God. Two wings covered their feet, this speaks of their great humility and reverence in their attendance upon God, and with two wings they made flight. These wings were kept ready for instant flight in the service of God. At the voice of God, the door post moved, and the house was filled with smoke, which represented the presence of God. Isaiah saw the Holiness of God and it changed his life. Perhaps if we were to preach more on the Holiness of God, more lives would be changed in our congregations. When we concentrate or meditate on the Holiness of God, it will cleanse our minds from our sins and problems and enable and empower us to worship Him and serve Him for who He is not for what we can get from Him.

My sister, believe God's Word. Preach it, live it, and may the love of God keep you in all your ways. Be blessed and be a blessing to those God has entrusted to you.

Chapter 12
WOMEN OF THE BIBLE

Throughout the Bible we find accounts of women who were used by God in various positions and circumstances. These were Spirit-filled women of God many who went beyond their normal lifestyle to accomplish their mission for God. We have included some of them along with a brief statement about their story. Please be encouraged as you use the reference to where their complete stories may be found in the Bible.

THE OLD TESTAMENT

Deborah: A great woman of God called by God to be a prophetess, as well as a judge during the time of judges. She was a woman of integrity, strength, and leadership. With more political power than any other woman in the Bible. Her relationship with God gave her the blessed ability to hear from and recognize the voice of God. In her obedience to God, she accompanied Barak into battle against King Jabin. You may read her story in Judges 4.

Ruth: An obedient woman of faith, humility, loyalty and courage. She moved beyond her familiar surroundings and homeland to follow her mother-in-law to a foreign land and by faith serve a God that she did not know. She was obedient to the leading of her mother-in-law and as a result, she is named in the genealogy of Jesus Christ. You may read about this story in the book of Ruth.

Huldah: A prophetess who dwelt in Jerusalem in the second quarter during the time King Josiah. She gave the word of the Lord to the servants of Josiah whom he had sent to her to inquire of a word from God. God used this great prophetess to deliver his word to a king and a nation. You may read of her story in II Kings 22:14-20.

Hannah: A great woman of prayer and faith. She prayed for a child, promised God to return him to God for His service. God heard her desperate prayer, responded to her faith and passion and He rewarded her faith by giving her a son whom she named Samuel. Samuel was used of God as a great prophet to accomplish God's will for Israel. You may read about Hannah in I Samuel 1 and I Samuel 2.

Esther: A bold and beautiful young lady who risked her life to save an entire nation. She acted in obedience to the request of her cousin, Mordecai, who had raised her as his own daughter. Esther stepped outside of the box to accomplish God's plan for His people. She fasted and sought wisdom from God to prepare her for this mission. She demonstrated great courage and obedience. You may read her story in the book of Esther.

THE NEW TESTAMENT

Anna: According to scripture, Anna, a prophetess, lived in the temple at Jerusalem, devoting her life to God. When Mary and Joseph came to the temple to dedicate baby Jesus, Anna was present. Through the Spirit, she recognized him as the long-awaited Messiah. From that moment on, she spoke of Jesus to those in Jerusalem who were looking for redemption. You may read Anna's story of faith in the promises of God in Luke 2:36-38.

Priscilla: The wife of Aquilla who partnered with her husband in ministry as a spokeswoman for the cause of Christ. She became a student of the Apostle Paul and under his teaching and mentoring. she became a great carrier of the word of God. She was instrumental in instructing Apollos in Christian faith. She along with her husband used their home as a church. You may find the accounts of Priscilla in Acts 18:2-3,26, Romans 16:3-4, and I Corinthians 16:19.

Mary Magdalene: Mary Magdalene represents a woman whose life was changed forever in spite of past mistakes. She became a faithful follower of Jesus after He delivered her from several demons. There are several particular events that relate to Mary Magdalene:

1. She remained at the cross for the entire time of Christ's crucifixion and followed to see where Jesus would be buried.
2. She was the first person to recognize Christ after His resurrection (see Mark 16:9).
3. She was the first person that Christ spoke to after His resurrection. He called her by her name (see John 20:16).
4. She was the first person to take the news of His resurrection to His disciples at His directions.

    You will find her story in all four Gospels: Matthew 27 and Matthew 28, Mark chapters 15 and 16, Luke chapters 23 and 24, and John 20.

Phoebe: A devout woman of God referred to by the Apostle Paul as a "servant." The word servant is usually translated "minister" when referring to men. Some believe Phoebe was a deaconess. Whatever her title, she helped to spread the gospel and offered her services, encouragement, and instructions to those to whom she ministered to in her hometown of Cenchrea. The Apostle Paul named her as one of his helpers and commended her to the church. You will find her story in Romans 16:1-3.

The Samaritan woman: This woman had an encounter with Jesus at Jacob's well in Samaria. She was a woman who had a bad reputation, but after her conversation with Jesus her life was changed. She received the Holy Spirit and became the first woman evangelist. She boldly took the news of her encounter with Jesus back to her town. A whole town came to know Jesus as a result of her testimony about Jesus. You may find her story in John 4:1-42.

Chapter 13

ON BEING SINGLE

It is my intention to cover as many topics as I thought would benefit women in ministry. It is to that extent that I believe it will be beneficiary to add this chapter "On Being Single." There are many women who are hearing the call of God on their lives who are single.

I am not single, so to help me in this area, I enlisted the help of one of my good friends who is single. She was formerly an assistant pastor and is currently contemplating starting a church. She is an experienced woman of God whom I have known for several years. I greatly respect her and her commitment to the call of ministry in her life. She is a dedicated woman of integrity, and I feel her experience will be of value to all my single sisters in ministry. I am extremely fortunate she agreed to share her opinions with us.

QUESTIONS AND RESPONSES

The questions I asked were about her experience in ministry and dating. I chose not to include her name for personal and private interest on her behalf.

Questions on Ministry:

1. **What challenges (if any) do you face that you attribute to being a single woman in ministry?**

In terms of challenges that I face and attribute to being a single woman in ministry, I would have to say that I feel that sometimes others may judge me for not understanding dating, marriage, and the opposite gender. While I may not fully understand, I strongly feel that when the Lord provides an opportunity for me to minister, He will give me special insight or rely on His Word to instruct and encourage His people.

2. **How do you handle those difficulties?**

I choose to handle these challenges by understanding that while I will never know every facet of the ins and outs of a relationship, I know what I know and what I don't know. Christ will reveal to me if He chooses to do so.

3. **Do you feel being single affects your ministry positively, negatively, or not?**

Because I am not married at this time, I am unsure how much or to what capacity singlehood impacts the ministry the Lord has entrusted to me. I will say that it has made me extremely cautious in terms of my "walk with Christ." I am extra careful how I dress and diligently aware of how I carry myself. I make endless efforts to be cognizant of how I act and how those of the opposite sex perceive me. While I believe every woman who proclaims Christ as Lord and Savior should be aware of these characteristics of women working for the Kingdom. I feel that single women in ministry have a heightened sense of duty.

4. **Is there a difference between the older and younger adults in their acceptance of your single status?**

It is sad to say that there is a difference between the attitudes of younger and older adults regarding my single status. It has been my experience that the younger people may wonder about it, but overall don't take issues with it, while the older adults sometimes treat those that have not been married past the age of thirty-five like they had some plague. Thus, I feel the younger adults are a bit more comfortable in the pastoral leadership position.

5. **Do you find there is a difference between men and women in their attitudes towards you based on your single status?**

It is very unusual for a woman my age to be single with no children. I prefer to use the word "peculiar" (as my former church mother used to refer to me for years when introducing me to someone). Upon learning of my single status, I have found that men, in general, will act as if I am some kind of challenge or quest to be conquered rather than just attempting to get to know me as any regular person would. On the other hand, older women are slightly different in their response to my single status and treat me with a "What is wrong with her? She needs to be fixed"—look or disposition. Younger women generally don't seem to be as bothered by it and could usually care less.

6. **Where do you find your most encouragement, mentors, friends, parents, or relatives besides your faith in God and Prayer?**

I attempt to find comfort and strength in older women, which has always proved to be a difficult task since most of them are married with children and grandchildren.

Questions on Dating:

1. **How important is dating to you, or is it not important?**

Dating is extremely important to me. It gives one the opportunity to know the potential marriage partner outside the environment surrounding the church setting. I am a firm believer that one cannot just discuss scripture all day but explore the likes and dislikes of one's future spouse. Examples of light topics could include their favorite types of movies, hobbies, and favorite types of food. Once the relationship becomes more serious, heavier subjects could be explored, such as one's ideology and respect for money, how one handles anger, one's future aspirations or goals, and the importance of family, to name a few. Dating should be a time of exploration to get to know oneself and the other party. They should view it with the overall goal of matrimony in a future sense.

2. **Do you date men who are part of a ministry in the church or ministers/pastors exclusively? Why or why not?**

    I choose to date men who have accepted Christ as their Lord and Savior and have no other desire than to serve and live for Him. Whether they are part of the clergy or not is immaterial to me. While I believe that men in the ministerial field will have more of an understanding of the strains that ministry can bring, I have no personal preference.

3. **Would you consider dating someone not serving in any capacity in the church? Yes, No, Why or Why not?**

    I sometimes feel the tendency of a man not to be in ministry will make me somewhat more grounded and normal, if that makes any sense. Again, I desire that he loves God and will honor me as I will honor him during our dating, engagement, and married life.

4. **Explain in your own words the difference between being alone and being lonely.**

    Sometimes, in pursuing the Master's Will, one can find oneself in a place of loneliness. While we are never fully alone in Christ, it may sometimes appear to be just that . . . ! I often remind myself through reading the Bible and through the encouragement of others that He is with me. He said in His Word that He would never leave or forsake us. He also said He would keep my mind in perfect peace if my mind is stayed on Him and if I trust him. I do seek to trust him. Despite feeling alone {and I am not), I also feel that there are periods or seasons when God would have us be alone to minister to us more intently and purposefully.

5. How do you handle either or both?

There are times in pastoral ministry and singlehood when loneliness is inevitable; sometimes, it stays longer than one would like it to. I attempt to find solace in the promises of God that He knows what is best for me at this present time in my life. I find comfort in those who accept me as a friend, not as a pastor, nor as someone who has spoken in conferences and been privileged to be an instrument God has used.

6. Do you have a desire to be married? Yes, No, not necessarily.

Desiring to be married is very important to me. It is truly the only way (other than the leading and instruction of God) that I will come to know my mate on a natural, emotional, and comical level. He must have a great sense of humor to deal with me (smile). I do desire to be married and trust that in the meantime, God knows what He is doing and that I should stay out of his way yet find and stay in the center of His Will.

General Question:

What advice would you offer single women in the ministry based on your experiences? Feel free to be generous in your words of encouragement.

> To those who remain single and are waiting for their "Prince Charming" in the natural, I say, "Hold On!" Don't compromise and allow the enemy to trick you into believing you should be treated with less than you deserve. Don't become desperate and accept anything that walks in a pair of pants. God knows you; you are fearfully and wonderfully made, and He has already created and masterfully planned the mate He has for you. Let Him escort you to your groom so you will look back and marvel at what He has done in the latter days. Until then, continue to strive daily to be not only a public success in the Lord but to strive equally as well not to be a private failure.

As I stated earlier, the answers provided are from the participant's experiences. They may not reflect your personal experiences/opinions. However, I feel the questions are "food for thought" for single women in Ministry. Perhaps these questions will invoke personal considerations/concerns that may be probable in Ministry.

Your response to this chapter should reflect your earnest self. Be true to you!!

Chapter 14

A FINAL WORD

Sisters, let us celebrate our strength as women who are called by God. Know who you are in Christ first!

Proverbs 27:17 says,

"As iron sharpens iron, so one man sharpens another."

Embrace the advice of a caring and trusting mentor. Their experience will be very beneficial to you as you move forward in your ministry. Be sure to let them know how much you appreciate them by your words and your actions. I've heard it said, "what comes from the heart reaches the heart." As you grow and mature in the ministry you, too, are being prepared to become mentors to the next generation of God's daughters who have been called to carry His Word.

We must all give honor and thanks to those sisters who were the trailblazers before us.

Those who forged ahead in spite of the difficulties they faced when the ceiling was solid. Those sisters who did not allow rejection to prevent them from doing what God called them to do. They were the ones who persevered and endured. They were the originals who loved God enough to withstand the rejection, not only from their male counterparts, but also from females who were being influenced and not ready for the change. Those were the sisters who virtually opened the doors for those of us who would come along long after many of them had been called home to receive their rewards as faithful servants.

We must also thank our male counterparts who have embraced the truth about women in ministry and always supported us with prayer and opportunity to preach from the pulpits in the churches they pastor, to the dismay and disapproval of their fellow brothers in ministry.

My ten years in the pastorate was quite a journey, however I would not exchange the experience for anything. I learned more about God, myself, and people in general during my tenure as pastor. I know that being called to the ministry in any capacity is a "special" gift from God. Even though the journey got rough at times, I can truly say that I know that God was with me all the way.

Now that I am retired from the pastorate, one of my favorite scriptures I embrace and pray often these days is from Psalm 71:17-18 (NKJV),

> "O God, You have taught me from my youth;
> and to this day I declare Your wondrous works.
> Now also when I am old and gray-headed, O God do not
> forsake me, Until I declare Your strength to this generation,
> Your power to everyone who is to come."

To this day, thankfully God continues to use the gift He placed in me.

God has taken me to a new level in the ministry. What He has prepared me to do now is what I call "uncharted territory," including His guidance and inspiration to write this book. My prayer is that my younger sisters will be able to use this work as a source of help and even comfort as they journey on the path called ministry.

Go forward my sisters and be blessed.

To God be the glory!

ABOUT THE AUTHOR

REV. CAROLYN A. COOKS is the former Senior Pastor of Sunnyside Baptist Church in Los Angeles, California. Before being installed as Pastor, she served as Associate Minister of Evangelism. Prior to her call in the ministry, she was also active in several auxiliaries at Sunnyside. She was a co-founder of the Youth and Young Adult Usher Board, where she served as a counselor and was a Sunday School teacher for more than twenty five years. She was the visionary of the Whole Women's Conference, part of the Women's Ministry at Sunnyside.

Pastor Cooks has been a guest speaker in the states of Texas and Oklahoma as well as a facilitator at conferences in and around the Los Angeles, Pasadena, and Antelope Valley, California areas. She identifies herself as a preacher/teacher, and she believes that Sunday School and Bible Study are the principle components of Christian growth.

Pastor Cooks is a former executive board member of the Lennox Clergy Council. During her time of participation in this council, she served as a member of a program sponsored by the Lennox Clergy Council, the Youth Accountability Board (a component of the Juvenile Justice Probation Department). She has received recognition from the American Red Cross for her participation in the ARC South Area Disaster Preparation Program. Pastor Cooks is also an honoree/recipient of several awards including The Top Ladies of Distinction Women of Excellence Award, the 2011 Meritorious Woman Award from the NAACP Los Angeles Youth Council, and The Wind Beneath my Wings Award from Athens B.C.

She served on the Ordination Council of The American Baptist Churches of Los Angeles. She is currently an honorary member of CCUNAT, a non-profit organization of Christian Pastors and laity, also the Gathering of Reverend Sisters, and is the first female pastor of an American Baptist Church of the Pacific Southwest.

Pastor Cooks is a graduate of Bethany Christian Bible College, where she received a certificate in Systematic Christian Education. She has a Bachelor's Degree in Biblical Studies and graduated (Magna-Cum-Laude) with a Master's Degree from M.T.I. Bible College in Los Angeles.

Although retired from the Pastorate, she continues being actively involved in Ministry, preaching and ministering at various churches and special events.

Pastor Cooks serves as a member of the Prayer Ministry at her home church in the Antelope Valley, the teacher for weekly Bible Study, and the Director of Christian Education. Her desire and prayer presently is inspired by Psalm 71:17-18,

"O God You have taught me from my youth;
And to this day I declare Your wondrous works.
(18) Now also when I am old and gray headed, O God, do not
forsake me, Until I declare Your Strength to this generation,
Your power to everyone who is to come."

BIBLIOGRAPHY

Building Credibility in Leadership, Author, Michael Blue, 2011, Creation House Books, A Charisma Media Company, Lake Mary, Florida.

"Teach My Hands to War" (Praise is a Weapon) Artist, Marvin L. Sapp, Written by Aron Lindsey, 2012.

Matthew Henry Commentary/New Modern Edition, 1991, Hendrickson Publishers, Inc., Peabody, Massachusetts.

The Charles F. Stanley Life Principles Bible, Author, Dr. Charles F. Stanley, 2005, Thomas Nelson, Inc., Nashville, Tennessee.

www.ingramcontent.com/pod-product-compliance
Lightning Source LLC
Chambersburg PA
CBHW051322120626
46547CB00015B/2349